Sound Beginnings

Learning and Development
in the Early Years

Also available:

Planning Children's Play and Learning in the Foundation Stage, second edition
Jane Drake
1 84312 151 4

Developing Early Years Practice
Linda Miller, Carrie Cable and Jane Devereux
1 84312 317 7

Planning and Using Time in the Foundation Stage
Jill Williams and Karen McInnes
1 84312 279 0

Sound Beginnings

Learning and Development
in the Early Years

PAMELA MAY, ERICA ASHFORD
and GILL BOTTLE

 David Fulton Publishers

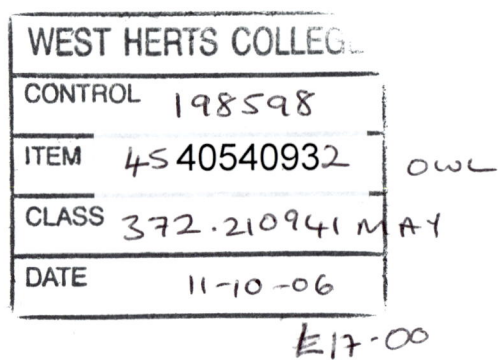
David Fulton Publishers Ltd
The Chiswick Centre, 414 Chiswick High Road, London W4 5TF

www.fultonpublishers.co.uk

First published in Great Britain in 2006 by David Fulton Publishers

10 9 8 7 6 5 4 3 2 1

David Fulton Publishers is a division of Granada Learning Limited.

British Library Cataloguing in Publication Data
A catalogue record for this book is available from the British Library.

ISBN: 1 84312 422 X
EAN: 9781843124221

Typeset by Servis Filmsetting Ltd, Manchester
Printed and bound in Great Britain

Contents

Acknowledgements

The authors wish to acknowledge the significant influence that Tricia David, Julie Fisher, Lesley Grundy and Biddy Youell have had on their professional lives. They have inspired the adults with whom they worked and empowered the children they taught.

We wish to thank those friends who have been interested in this project and our families for their love and encouragement. In particular we wish to thank John May for his editorial help and Anne Nurse for taking the photographs that support the text. They were taken at Comper, Headington and Slade Nursery Schools in Oxford.

Every effort has been made to trace copyright holders of material reproduced in this book. Any right not acknowledged here will be acknowledged in subsequent printings if notice is given to the publishers.

About the authors

Pamela May is a senior lecturer in early years at Canterbury Christchurch University. She currently teaches on Foundation Degrees and Early Childhood Studies programmes. She has been a nursery teacher, head teacher and co-ordinator of a specialist early years PGCE.

Erica Ashford is a senior lecturer in the Department of Childhood Studies at Canterbury Christchurch University. She has studied at the Tavistock Clinic and has a postgraduate diploma in psychology and an MA in children's literature.

Gill Bottle is a senior lecturer in the Department of Education at the University of Gloucester. She teaches on a range of QTS courses and is responsible for those courses based on the Foundation Stage. Her doctoral studies interrogated the links between early mathematical experiences in the home and those at school. She is the author of *Maths 3–11*.

All I really need to know I learned in kindergarten

All I really need to know about how to live and what to do and how to be I learned in kindergarten. Wisdom was not at the top of the graduate school mountain, but there in the sandpile at Sunday School. These are the things I learned. Share everything. Play fair. Don't hit people. Put things back where you found them. Clean up your own mess. Don't take things that aren't yours. Say you're sorry when you hurt somebody. Wash your hands before you eat. Flush. Warm cookies and milk are good for you. Live a balanced life – learn some and think some and draw and paint and sing and dance and play and work every day some. Take a nap every afternoon.

When you go out into the world, watch out for traffic, hold hands, and stick together. Be aware of wonder. Remember the little seed in the Styrofoam cup: the roots go down and the plant goes up and nobody really knows how or why, but we are all like that. Goldfish and hamsters and white mice and even the little seed in the Styrofoam cup – they all die. So do we.

Everything you need to know is in there somewhere. The Golden Rule and love and basic sanitation. Ecology and politics and equality and sane living. Take any of those items and extrapolate it into sophisticated adult terms and apply it to your family life or your work or your government or your world and it holds true and clear and firm. Think what a better world it would be if all the whole world had cookies and milk about three o'clock every afternoon and then lay down with our blankies for a nap. Or if all governments had a basic policy to always put things back where they found them and to clean up their own mess. And it is still true, no matter how old you are when you go out into the world, it is best to hold hands and stick together.

(Taken from *All I really need to know I learned in Kindergarten* by Robert Fulghum. New York: Ballantine Books, 1990)

Introduction

Two major beliefs underpin this book. The first is that the role of the early years educator is complex and challenging and the second is the notion of the child as a powerful and competent learner.

These beliefs are reflected in the Qualifications and Curriculum Authority's *Curriculum Guidance for the Foundation Stage* (QCA 2000). For example, we are reminded that 'although teaching can be defined simply, it is a complex process' (p. 22) and, on page 14, there is the expectation that children will 'initiate their own learning' (p. 14) and that adults will 'allow time for sustained concentration' (p. 20). Children are acknowledged as being already skilled and experienced learners by the time they reach our settings. Our task is the hugely challenging but rewarding one of being a partner on their learning journey.

The purpose of this book is to celebrate the spirit of the Foundation Stage. The first 27 pages of the *Curriculum Guidance* exemplify the principles that are the core of each chapter of this book. In its advice on 'learning', 'teaching' and 'play' it describes settings that are 'stimulating' and children who spend their time 'exploring, investigating, discovering, creating, revising, consolidating and rehearsing'. It is anticipated that this will be done most effectively 'through playing and talking' (p. 20).

This section of the *Guidance* is not content-led but instead clearly defines the processes which enable young children to learn effectively. It seemed timely, therefore, after the *Guidance* had been in operation for five years, to read current research and listen to anecdotal evidence from early years education advisers and from our own students who are practitioners to discover what influence the *Guidance* was having on practice.

It is with growing concern, therefore, that the authors, in their roles as teacher educators and lecturers, recognise a significant gap between what they are teaching and the everyday experiences of practitioners and students in early years settings. The document appears sometimes to be used in settings as a manual rather than as curriculum guidance, with the Areas of Learning and Early Learning

Goals section providing little more than ideas for use in helping to complete the assessment profile.

This, we know, was never the intention. If the powerful statements of the first sections of the document are fully understood, with their emphasis on play and child-initiated learning, then practitioners are empowered to work in imaginative and responsive ways. The Stepping Stones section was designed to be used as a scaffold to support and guide the emerging understanding of newly trained practitioners, or practitioners new to the Foundation Stage, and to explain the progressive nature of learning. As their confidence and experience grows they should be able to progress beyond this section and teach creatively and holistically using their own formulated principles as guidance.

This book restates principles that have an honourable history in early years tradition, having been a part of Sir Christopher Ball's Startright Report (Ball 1994) and adapted by Tina Bruce in her book *Early Childhood Education* (Bruce 1987).

These principles reappear in a similar format in the *Curriculum Guidance for the Foundation Stage* (QCA 2000: 11–13) and make an interesting starting point

---

FUNDAMENTAL PRINCIPLES OF GOOD PRACTICE

1 Early childhood is the foundation upon which children build the rest of their lives.

2 Children develop at different rates and in different ways.

3 All children have abilities which should be identified and promoted.

4 Young children learn from everything that happens to them and around them.

5 Children learn most effectively through actions rather than instructions.

6 Children learn best when they are actually involved and interested.

7 Children who feel confident about themselves and their own ability have a head start in learning.

8 Children need time and space to produce work of quality and depth.

9 Play and conversation are the main ways in which children learn about themselves and others.

10 Children who are encouraged to act for themselves are more likely to act independently.

11 The relationships which children make with other children and adults are of central importance in their development.

12 What children can do should be the starting point for their learning.

Everything I need to know . . .

for the formation of a 'manifesto' or 'reasons why' for learning and teaching, setting out why things should happen in certain ways. The strength of basing early years practice on principles is that principles are researched, tried and tested and known to accord with how children develop. They therefore remain a constant and provide evidence in a world where new and different strategies are frequently being imposed on the professional workforce. These varying strategies are well meant, but tend to emanate from a negative concept of the young child as incompetent and dependent. They tend to be based on projects and pilots, but not often on robust research.

An additional worry is that many practitioners seem to be unclear about the implications of child development for their practice and, indeed, to have only a hazy notion of the concept itself. Without a deep knowledge of child development, they are tempted to move young children forward quickly to formal pencil and paper based learning where results can be easily assessed and measured, thus perpetuating the notion of the incompetent child. Children will, of course, display incompetence if required to learn in inappropriate ways. Even if practitioners are clear about their practice, it is often hard for them to be confidently articulate about more loosely structured ways of learning, which are playful and which require them to share control and responsibilities with very young children.

This book aims to give students and practitioners some knowledge, strategies and confidence to help them to teach by their principles. We hope that these principles will empower them to question any demands made on them to work in ways that are inappropriate. We hope that they will feel able to regularly ask themselves 'Why am I teaching in this way?' and 'Is it appropriate for these children?' By becoming articulate and reflective they will be able to talk with confidence to families and other colleagues about their work. Practitioners who are clear about their practice and eager to share their view of young children as strong and powerful will be well respected by the community in which they work as their settings will be good places for children to be.

Each chapter of the book reflects one or two of the principles described above. The suggestion is that if the principles are understood, then the practice might reflect them in the ways discussed. In other words: 'If you believe in this, then your setting might look like this.'

Each chapter starts by stating the original principle, and is followed by the authors' ideas as to how they see the principle(s) applying to practice. At the end of each chapter there are two points for reflection. The first asks the reader to examine their own beliefs and to use this reflection to formulate a strand of a professional ethos. This may be quite removed from the day-to-day reality of the setting. The second question asks how the principle could be incorporated into practice.

We fully appreciate that it has not been possible to separate out principles discretely and that ideas have flowed through the text in a holistic way, rather as good early years practice does. However, the hope is that these ideas may provide starting points for students and practitioners to reflect on and discuss their practice and that these reflections and discussions may embolden all those effective practitioners to be courageous in their provision of challenging learning experiences for children.

In the authors' current roles of teaching early years practice it is evident that greater response and understanding comes from those students who have had experience with young children either at home or in a setting. Many of us went through our training with a barest nod in the direction of much of what is in this book. So this book is both for the new trainee, as it aims to re-enforce the importance of educational theory and to point to how it links to practice, and also for the early years professional who may not have been trained as a specialist in the field and yet finds themselves working with the very youngest children. We hope that this book will help all those professionals to ensure that children in early years settings receive appropriate education and care which is of the highest quality, taught through a full curriculum and which is based on sound educational principles.

References

Ball, C. (1994) *The Importance of Early Learning* (Startright Report). London: Royal Society of Arts.

Bruce, T. (1987) *Early Childhood Education*. Sevenoaks: Hodder and Stoughton.

QCA (2000) *Curriculum Guidance for the Foundation Stage*. London: QCA.

Foundations

A background to early years education

Wise educators have always worked with children in ways that match current understanding of how children learn best. Practitioners have been trained, therefore, to observe children carefully so that what they plan is based on a secure knowledge of what children can already do or can nearly do. It is common good practice to build on children's interests, valuing their experiences, and to respect the skills that they have already gained before or outside our setting. Current early years tradition derives from the Kindergarten movement which so aptly translates as 'the garden of children'. The most influential early years educators of the twentieth century such as Rachel and Margaret McMillan, Susan Isaacs and Robert Owen recognised the need to provide nourishing environments for children's minds, bodies and spirits, which would give children the best chance to thrive.

The notion that children's early experience is a profound indicator of their subsequent success as older children and, later, as adults has been growing in strength over the last hundred years. It reached a decisive point in the long-term Headstart research in the USA which began in the 1960s. This research continues to provide conclusive evidence that money spent by governments on high quality early educational experiences pays dividends by reducing the costs to society in supporting families struggling with crime, unwanted pregnancies, drug abuse and unemployment. In fact, so powerful was this message from the USA that the current government's early years agenda has been influenced by the positive messages that have come from the American Headstart experience. In this country we have seen the introduction of early intervention projects such as SureStart and Peers Early Education Partnership (PEEP) based on this under-standing of the value of early education experiences. The international journal *Early Years Education* reported in 2003 that New Zealand researchers, in the 'Competent Child' study, found that children who had three or more years of early childhood education had higher scores in maths, communication, problem solving and reading and writing at age ten. These results complement those from the 'Effective Provision of Preschool Education' (EPPE) project which identified effective provision by linking child development to children's experiences in a range of early years settings.

However, these ideas have not gone unchallenged. In this country, since the early 1980s the education of young children has been subjected to a number of constraints which led to a narrowing of children's experiences and a formalisa-tion of practice which, it is now clear, did not serve society well in the business of producing creative and independent citizens. This practice derived from the 'skills and drills' approach was first used in the board schools of the nineteenth century and had much to do with providing a numerate and literate workforce and little to do with education.

Perhaps the area of greatest controversy has been the view of so many theor-ists that play has a valid place in educational settings and is a valuable tool for learning. The exciting ideas that have been emerging from the field of neuro-science appear to support the 'kindergarten' approach to learning in highlighting the role that stimulating, playful experiences have in the formation of the healthy brain.

The foundations upon which children's lives are built are also influenced by a country's national history. The schools in the Reggio Emilia district of northern Italy developed their philosophy of children's independence of thought as a direct result of Italy's leader, Mussolini. Loris Malaguzzi, who founded the trad-ition of schooling which promotes creativity, collaboration and autonomy, was convinced that a people who thought independently and creatively would not be easily oppressed and dominated. This complemented the notion of communal responsibility, which varies from country to country and has had a significant impact on provision for both care and education. Whereas many other societies take communal responsibility for the early years and provide state-funded educa-tion for all their very young, in England the family has traditionally assumed this role, leading to what Margaret Thatcher referred to as a 'rich patchwork of provision' when she was minister for education in the 1970s.

As can be the case with patchwork, the quality, though varied and interesting, was uneven, with many children, particularly in rural areas, offered little choice of provision and few trained early years practitioners.

The current scene

The *Curriculum Guidance for the Foundation Stage*, which was published in 2000, is a document that celebrates the importance of this early stage in children's lives as being the basis on which the rest of their lives are built. Its philosophy underpins what a range of professionals are now telling us. It confirms that it is vital to create an environment around children which fosters good health, a positive disposition to learning and positive self-image, good social skills and a good balance between dependence and inter-dependence. The *Guidance* recognised that young children have huge potential and encouraged practitioners to see them as active and competent learners who 'have a wide range of skills and interests'. Children would spend their time engaged in 'rich and stimulating experiences' alongside adults who 'use encouraging, friendly, optimistic and lively approaches to support children' (QCA 2000: 8, 23).

Alongside this document came significant government funding in recognition of a state responsibility to provide care and education for our youngest children and alongside funding came accountability. It is the nature of this accountability, in the form of inspection criteria and measurable outcomes, with their emphasis on literacy and numeracy, that has sapped the confidence of many practitioners. It has led some of them to mistake the *Curriculum Guidance for the Foundation Stage* as a manual with a set of boxes to tick rather than a set of guidelines to support their professional expertise. A young boy in a setting recently responded to questioning about the car he was playing with by saying 'It's blue and it's got four wheels'. Considerable further prompting got a more enthusiastic follow-up. The car was called a Porsche and had heated seats, just like his granddad's car. Here was a child who was conditioned to assessment which concentrated on 'Does he know his colours and numbers to five?', rather than a strategy of engaging with his interests to foster a rich use of language. Clearly this boy's engagement in describing his experience with his blue car could have been much more 'rich and stimulating'.

Children's potential

Children's belief in their own potential to be explorers, to be friends, to communicate, to construct their own meaning and to develop a sense of fairness depends largely on the response of those adults with whom they regularly come into contact. If those adults believe that these early experiences lay down the ground rules for children's belief in themselves, they will ensure that their settings are full of conversations about Porsches with heated seats and less about blue cars with four wheels.

What, then, do we understand that young children can do, given an environment which supports and understands them? Table 1.1 shows a list compiled by the Early Years Curriculum Group (1996) which, by its range, indicates the wealth of potential skills to be found in four-year-old children.

Table 1.1 Potential skills of four-year-olds (in no particular order)

Develop independence	Learn through being active	Construct their own meaning
Assert themselves	Be physically confident	Make sense of the world
Learn to collaborate and co-operate	Be quiet and reflective at times	Learn very fast
Form a wider network of relationships	Refine their motor skills	Develop a sense of humour
Develop positive self-identity and self-esteem	Learn through all their senses	Concentrate on things that are interesting and meaningful to them
Be concerned about honesty and fairness, and open to questions of equality	Be curious and exploratory	Question and reason
Take responsibility for themselves and their actions	Develop knowledge about their bodies	Understand and accept the need for rules
Begin to take responsibility for others	Extend their physical capabilities	Be linguistically competent – as talkers, listeners, mark makers, storytellers and readers
Develop a sense of right and wrong	Learn how to use a wide range of tools and equipment	Categorise and make comparisons
Respond to stimulation with enthusiasm and wonder	Make conceptual connections	Build learning from familiar situations
Display caring and empathy	Observe carefully	Learn from others

(published in Oxfordshire Curriculum Matters No 13, 1996, OCC, Oxford)

The garden of childhood

The list is in no particular order but offers a reminder of the cognitive, physical, emotional, spiritual, moral and creative dimensions that should be considered when planning for children's development. By its breadth it reminds us that there is much more to education than academic bodies of knowledge.

While creating a 'cave' by covering a climbing frame with blankets, the practitioner can plan activities and provision with the children which will allow for a full range of developmental possibilities. Thought can be given not only to academic potential such as the science of creating light in the dark cave but also to questions of fearfulness of the dark and which senses can be used in the dark. Many young children have never seen the night-time sky because of the increase in urban lighting and respond with wonder if their attention is drawn to stars and planets. A glance at the list will reveal a wide range of opportunities to support children's potential as a thinker, a social, moral and emotional being and a member of the community beyond the family who is in the process of making themselves at home in the wider world.

A rich and stimulating environment

This 'rich and stimulating environment' lies at the heart of good early years practice and is based on the common-sense understanding that if the practitioner

The lone scientist

finds interesting, stimulating and curious things in the setting, then the children will as well. Interested children are not only far too busy to be disruptive but also likely to demonstrate a wide range of physical, emotional and cognitive attributes which will develop more quickly if their efforts are valued and adult expectations are high yet achievable.

It is this unshakable belief that children can achieve their potential if given interesting things to learn about in an environment where they are supported by knowledgeable and committed adults that makes working in the early years such a rewarding profession. One of the first attitudes that the new early years practitioner needs to adopt is an encouragement for children to succeed. This 'can do' approach to their achievements helps success to build on success, as opposed to the more negative view of early childhood in which it is seen as a time when children demonstrate all the things they cannot do, such as reading, writing, addition and subtraction. A prerequisite of sound practice is that children are allowed to try things out, perhaps get them wrong, and to take some risks so that they can experiment in a safe but challenging environment. The setting that supports early learners best is that where both children and adults feel they belong and where they are enthusiastic about what is on offer.

Having accepted the concept of the young learner as competent and having recognised the importance of a child's early learning experiences in predicting later success, what strategies does the practitioner use to turn theory into practice and enable the young chid to learn most effectively? It is at this point that theorists help the practitioner make some everyday decisions about what the setting should look like and how resources can be used to encourage successful learning.

The process of learning

Fundamental to good practice is Jean Piaget's theory that children piece together their own understanding of the world from their individual experiences of it. He referred to children as 'lone scientists' who actively construct meaning from their everyday lives. This idea of 'active' rather than 'passive' learning has its roots in the theories of Jean-Jacques Rousseau and explains why children are either moving around or actively engaged for much of their time in a good early years setting. Some of Piaget's views of children as learners have been rightly challenged but his view of the child as actively constructing their own understanding remain a cornerstone of good practice. As Susan Isaacs (1932) so wisely advised: 'When we ask children not to move we should have excellent reasons for doing so. It is the stillness we have to justify, not the movement.' Active learning, then, will be a fundamental principle which governs how the setting is organised and the teaching done.

The idea of children constructing their own individual view of the world, or 'cognitive jigsaw' as it is sometimes known, is another fundamental principle that will influence how a setting is organised. It has far-reaching implications for the practitioner. It implies a role of a sharing of knowledge and understandings rather than a dispensing of it. It requires the child to retain a degree of ownership of what they are learning, which enables concepts to be securely embedded. This 'learning by doing' is accepted as being more effective than 'learning by looking' not only for very young children but for adults too. In just the same way that adults cannot pass the driving test by reading the *Highway Code*, children cannot learn about what floats and what sinks by completing worksheets about it. They need to try it out for themselves and then practise it again and again until the concepts are clearly understood.

Piaget's theory that learning was a solitary experience has been superseded by those of Lev Vygotsky and Jerome Bruner. Both believed learning to be a sociable activity and considered that the role of the 'expert other' is crucial to a child's success.

Vygotsky suggested that children could be thought of as 'cultural apprentices' and that language and communication are key aspects of successful learning.

Certainly some of the richest learning experiences that children have in settings would seem to involve elements that are both social and communicative; think perhaps of the 'what if' games in the role-play area or the guiding suggestions of the practitioner to 'try it this way' when the Sellotape gets tangled up in the workshop.

What a child can do unaided is described by Vygotsky as their 'zone of actual development' and the adult or expert other who supports the child at that point enables the learner to reach the next level, or their 'zone of proximal development'. Sarah, aged just four, comes into contact with a drill at the woodwork bench for the first time and correctly guesses, from her previous knowledge of handles and wheels, that turning the handle is part of what drills are about. Trudi, her nursery nurse, encloses Sarah's hands in her own and says, 'That's right, Sarah, put the end of the drill on the wood and turn the handle and you will drill a hole.' A few minutes later, with this sensitive support, Sarah joyfully holds up the piece of wood and shouts, 'I can see through it!' As the practitioner sees that less and less support is needed, she withdraws and Sarah gradually becomes more independent at the woodwork bench. Her 'actual development zone' is now using the drill unaided, though she will need considerably more practice before she can be called competent at this skill.

Jerome Bruner supports this view of the sociable learner who needs either an adult or a more knowledgeable child to 'scaffold' their progress. One of the essential, and sometimes missing, implications of Bruner's notion of 'scaffolding' is that there must be new learning available and that it must be available consistently for children to practise regularly and achieve competence. In practice, the woodwork skills of drilling, sawing and hammering nails will take a long while to refine and will only be achieved if thought and planning is given to how the activity is to be organised, resourced and staffed, based on these theories and principles.

Bruner also described a 'play spiral' which allows a child to join an activity at their current level of development and then revisit it with increased knowledge and experience, thus becoming more expert with each encounter. Sometimes, a mistaken notion that young children have short concentration spans can lead practitioners to change provision too readily, thus thwarting the child's need to practise and refine the skills they have just begun to explore. Sarah will not become proficient at drilling if the woodwork bench is only available once a week. New provision inevitably invites children to join it at the exploratory stage of learning, while developing competence and skill and revisiting the play spiral at a higher level requires existing provision to be maintained and extended to allow children to become proficient. An adult analogy might be the driving school instructor who provides a Ford Fiesta for the first driving lesson and a Mercedes automatic for the second! The unfortunate learner driver will stand little chance of gaining confidence and competence if the opportunity to build on existing knowledge is denied.

The learning process in practice

These theories, then, give practitioners pointers to consider. They all, in their different ways, subscribe to children learning most effectively when they are learning actively (Piaget), interactively (Vygotsky, Bruner) and independently (Piaget).

When children are learning actively, interactively and independently they are usually learning effectively. What might they be seen doing? They will most probably be communicating, experimenting, exploring, making decisions, problem solving and reflecting. When children are learning in these ways the setting looks busy and the children look engaged. Ferre Laevers has described children learning effectively as looking like 'fish in water' and this is certainly a powerful description of high quality practice. The implication for the practitioner is to think through each planned activity to be offered to ensure that children can use it in active, interactive and independent ways. Areas of the provision will, of course, vary in the ways in which they are used; some will be more interactive than others: the group of children building a tower with bricks, for example, is more interactive an activity by its nature than the child looking at a favourite book. This said, the richest provision will enable children to learn in these three ways and be available long enough for them to revisit the activity with increased understanding. All provision should engage children's interest so that they can connect with what is on offer and say to themselves 'Yes, I can do that'.

If provision is open-ended and flexible in its design then it is more likely that the majority of children will find a 'way in'. One autumn morning, for example, a spider had been made in the workshop by a practitioner and a group of children following the *Very Hungry Spider* story. The children's interest will persist if, one day, it is suggested that perhaps the spider needs a web which could be constructed in a corner of the setting. Then flies could be designed and made for the spider's breakfast, which could then be attached to the web to be followed by a letter from the spider thanking the children for their kindness! A correspondence of many weeks may well ensue if each letter is answered (by hard-working staff!). Children's enthusiasm to put pencil to paper will be long-lasting as the only expectation the spider has is that a name appears somewhere on the correspondence enabling her to reply. Children, if allowed to access this learning at a level relevant to them, will be motivated to succeed and will progress to ever more complex letters and ever more ingenious designs for flies!

Successful learning

Returning to the theme of successful learning, it will be seen that children engaged in this type of learning will, during the course of their writing and designing, be exploring, communicating, reflecting and experimenting. They will also be learning actively, interactively and independently. As success builds on success, children learning in this way will develop the notion that they are 'can-do' people.

The advantage with this type of flexible learning is that it recognises the value of the current stage of the child's development and interest and is not hooked into the aim of preparing the young child for the next stage of their life. Too often the Foundation Stage of learning is seen as a preparation for 'big school' or Key Stage 1 and much thought is given as to how best to prepare four- and five-year-old children for the next stage of their lives. It is a truism that the best way to prepare them for the next stage is to provide activities and learning that are appropriate for their current level of understanding so that what they are asked to do builds on what they can already, or nearly, do and not on what they cannot yet do. Failure and disaffection is caused by children being expected to learn and record learning in ways that are inappropriate to their levels of development, in the mistaken belief that this is the best way to prepare them for what lies ahead.

A definition of a high quality learning experience is hard to achieve as it is dependent on factors such as the ages and interests of children in the setting and the nature of the community from which they come. However, the following are useful questions for the practitioner to ask when deciding on provision or an activity:

- Does it arouse curiosity? Will children ask questions such as, 'What is it?', 'What does it do?' or 'What can I do with it?'
- Can it be used flexibly and in open-ended ways?
- Can it be available for a long time?
- Is it of good quality (not necessarily expensive) material?
- Can it be used by children at different levels of understanding and development?

If the answer is 'yes' to these questions, it is likely that children learning in this setting will enjoy a sense of achievement, well-being and raised self-esteem.

Activities and provision

One way of planning learning around what children have achieved or nearly achieved is to think of the setting as 'provision based' rather than 'activity based'. 'Activities' tend, by their nature, to be adult planned and led and to have learning objectives and outcomes. Provision, on the other hand, although planned and resourced by the adults, contains a range of learning opportunities with object-ives and outcomes that are usually inside children's minds. Sarah's delight at making a hole in her piece of wood when using the drill was that much more meaningful to her because it was *her* aim and she had clear ownership of the task. Happily, children's aims are often similar to the practitioner's, particularly if the provision has been sensitively and thoughtfully planned. The motivation, however, is increased a hundredfold if children can see their own aims being successfully accomplished. Intrinsic motivation and self-esteem are powerful drivers of effort and persistence.

If most of what the setting offers are learning experiences that are tightly tied to adults' objectives and outcomes, children's opportunities to build on what they know they can do and can nearly do is limited. What is to be learned is inside the practitioner's head rather than in the child's head and this also limits children's ability to think laterally and learn creatively. A sensitive balance between activities that are adult led and provision that is child initiated gives children the opportunity to show practitioners what levels of development they have reached and to demonstrate their interests and competencies. As an example, take Alan. He is a four-year-old with possible learning difficulties. Having shown little interest in the spider clinging to its web for several days, he was observed in the workshop carefully constructing a fly from a cork, Sellotape and two pieces of paper. He ran across to the web and hung his fly on to it, laughing. Until that point no adults had known that he was interested in this part of the provision or had appreciated his advanced level of understanding and competence that had enabled him to achieve such success. This knowledge was invaluable to the practitioners because, with little language, communication had been hard and planning for his learning not as accurate as they had wished. By using open-ended provision with no fixed outcomes, Alan felt he could contribute without fear of failure. His delight and confidence was a joy to see. Staff now had a clearer idea of how to plan for his learning and realised that they had been significantly underestimating his abilities.

The balance between 'activities' and 'provision' is a delicate one and made all the more complex as it involves decisions about issues of control. New and less confident practitioners often feel that they must be in control of all that happens in the setting. This appears as a 'top-down' model of learning with children tightly controlled, perhaps journeying around a carousel of activities or spending long periods of time sitting passively on the carpet during whole-group sessions. Some settings divide blocks of time into 'work' and 'play'. We have heard of settings that 'do HighScope in the afternoons'. These arrangements do little to reflect principles of good early years practice and inevitably restrict children's creative learning opportunities rather than open them up. The practitioner who has a secure understanding of and belief in these principles will have the courage to share ownership of the learning with the children by encouraging provision to be used in a variety of ways, valuing their ideas and following their leads.

Practitioners are, of course, in overall control and are responsible for all that happens in their setting, but what they need to consider is how to control aspects such as resources, time, staffing and levels of interaction and leave the ideas to the children, who will have no shortage of them!

A secure understanding of child development is key to planning an effective environment with provision that is engaging and appropriate to the levels of development the young child has reached. A knowledge of how children's development progresses from one stage to the next, together with a belief that the Foundation Stage of children's education is primarily practical in nature, gives professionals a sound basis upon which to plan and assess appropriate concepts and skills. *What* to teach during the Foundation Stage is very clearly laid down in England, unlike other countries which have chosen more wide-ranging curricula, but *how* to teach it depends on the individual practitioners' beliefs and understandings. There is much debate currently about the validity of teaching to children's stages of development (Dahlberg and Moss 1999). There are concerns that development is wrongly considered as inevitably linear and that children's cultural identity is in danger of being lost in the universality of such a theory. Nevertheless, the basic premise holds true, which is that on the way to learning a new piece of knowledge, there are steps which take the learner from practical exploration to expertise, competence and internalisation. It is the skill of observing where the learner is along this route and providing both opportunities to practise the emerging understanding and opportunities to try out the next step which defines the good practitioner.

Child development and good practice

A sound grasp of child development is acknowledged as being fundamental to good practice in the early years. However, in our experience of working with new and trainee practitioners, the concept is often not securely understood and therefore not incorporated into planning. Added to which, if current thinking is suggesting that development may be more holistic and cultural than linear, there seem to be even fewer certainties to cling to. A helpful way to think of a child's development may be to consider a Venn diagram with the major areas of development – cognitive, social/emotional and physical – overlapping (see Figure 1.1).

This moves us away from a linear model and yet accounts for progression from one level to another. It highlights the notion of the more complex aspects of children's activity needing to engage more than one area of their development. The more complex the learning, the more aspects of child development will be needed to complete a task. Simple motor skills, for example, such as jumping, hopping and running, are signs of a level of achievement. They

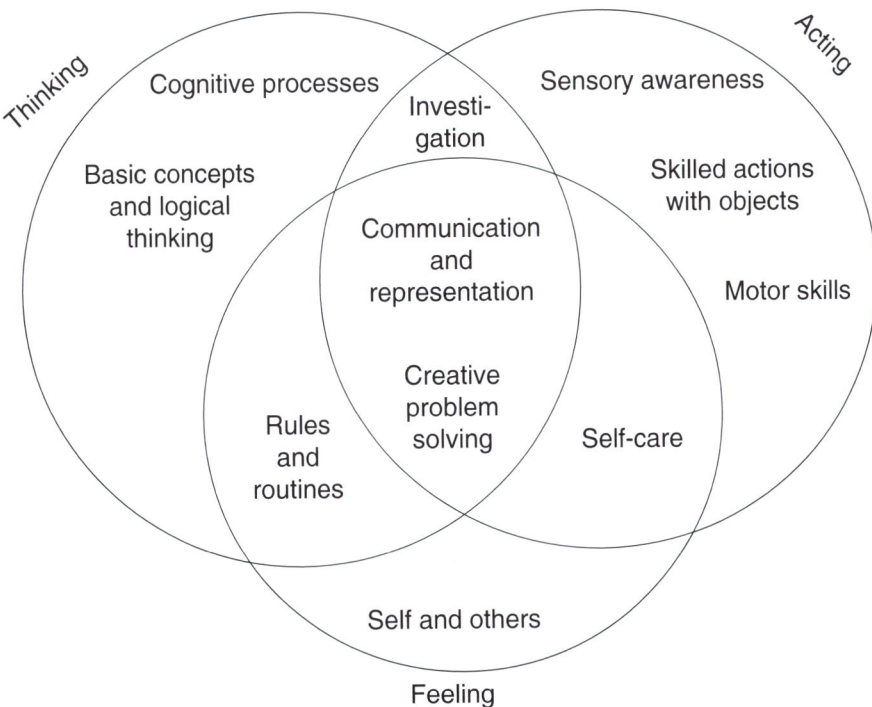

Figure 1.1 Areas of child development

become much more complex, however, when linked to other areas of development such as cognitive processes which would enable a child to use both their thinking skills and their motor skills to devise, perhaps, a treasure trail through the garden. The child, Alan, seen constructing the fly in the workshop was using not only his motor skills to construct the fly and his cognitive processes to think through the idea of using a cork, Sellotape and paper to make the fly, but also his emotional skills in having the motivation and self-confidence to put his plan into action. It was the complexity of what he achieved that gave the adults in the setting such joy, as their understanding of child development gave them a realistic picture of his abilities.

When children are engaged in representational activities or are investigating, communicating or solving problems creatively they are inevitably using the full range of their developmental skills. It is these children that Tina Bruce (1991) refers to as 'wallowing' in thoughts, feelings and ideas. They are operating at a high level of learning. It is this type of learning which is stimulating, rich and effective and which we should be offering to young children to motivate them to succeed.

Amir was excited by the spider hanging from her web in the corner of the setting and had listened attentively to the story. He was determined to receive a letter from the spider but was at the early stages of mark-making and unsure how to proceed when he saw other children posting pieces of paper into the spider's postbox. The practitioner suggested that he draw a picture for the spider, which he did with enthusiasm. He added the 'A' from his name and asked an adult to, add the other letters. Safe in the knowledge that the spider would know who to reply to, he happily posted his letter in the postbox and was rewarded with a reply the following morning. The nature of this provision also allowed Harriet to write letters at *her* developmental level. She had been writing with confidence for a few months and wrote each day to the spider to tell her what had been happening in her life. 'Yesterday I went to my Nan's' was followed by 'I've made you a fly biscuit' and 'I like spiders now', all of which taxed the spider's powers of creative authorship! The strength of this area of provision was that it encouraged creative writing in very young children at a range of levels to accommodate children's varying levels of skill and understanding. No child could fail and most were motivated to try to communicate by writing. Again, the phrase in the child's head is 'Yes, I can do that!' This approach of building on what children can do or can nearly do emphasises the 'competency' model rather than the 'deficit' model which emphasises what children can not yet do. The difficulty in pedagogical terms is that once a curriculum emphasises outcome measures it is the deficit model that predominates as the mismatch between sometimes inappropriate outcome measures and children's achievements becomes apparent. External outcome measures are sometimes set too high but are often too low, leaving children unable to find activities and provision to challenge and interest them. By moving away from measuring children's success in terms of cognitive and developmental achievements and measuring instead attitudes towards learning such as persistence, problem-solving abilities, creative thinking, collaboration and communication skills, we would surely be offering to the world young people with rich tools for success. It was Sir Christopher Ball who in 1994 defined the 'super skills of learning as motivation, social skills and high self-esteem'. We are well placed in the Foundation Stage setting to offer these through thoughtful and challenging provision.

Conclusion

In this chapter we have considered the importance of giving children a rich and stimulating environment as this will encourage their interest in the world. Early education needs to be seen as valuable in its own right and not solely as a preparation for stages to come. We have recognised that the child is a competent learner and that teaching should be based on what they can do rather than what they can not.

POINTS FOR REFLECTION

Yourself

Some people believe that early learning is primarily a training for the next stage of development. Others see it as a nourishing environment for children's minds, bodies and spirits in its own right. What is your view?

Your practice

How far does your setting's environment encourage children to explore and develop their own ideas?

References

Ball, C. (1994) *The Importance of Early Learning* (Startright Report). London: Royal Society of Arts.

Bruce, T. (1991) *Time to Play in Early Years Education*. London: Hodder and Stoughton.

Dahlberg, G. and Moss, P. (1999) *Beyond Quality in Early Years Education*. London: Routledge Falmer.

Isaacs, S. (1932) *The Children We Teach*. London: University of London Press.

QCA (2000) *Curriculum Guidance for the Foundation Stage*. London: QCA.

Active learning

The status of play

Play has often had a bad press in educational settings. Despite the positive tone in the *Curriculum Guidance for the Foundation Stage* which exhorts practitioners to 'extend and support children's spontaneous play', it seems much harder to implement in practice when faced with current demands for accountability and outcome measures.

Perhaps a good place to begin a consideration of play in educational settings would be with one of the great gurus of playful learning, Jerome Bruner. In an essay he proposed the notion that hunter-gatherer species had little use for formal instruction. The passing on of knowledge was functional and happened alongside the activity. 'The child was not drawn aside and told how to do it; he was shown while the action was going on' (Bruner 1976). Technological advances and the formalisation of schooling have increasingly disassociated action from knowledge and turned the gaining of knowledge from a process of 'knowing how' into a process of 'knowing that'. In subsequent studies with Sylva and Genova (1976) Bruner explored the idea that playful ways of learning helped children to solve problems more effectively than if they were taught the answers in a more formal, decontextualised way. Their experiments were with groups of young children who were given objects which would help them solve a specific problem. One group were shown (taught) how to use the objects, the other group were allowed to use them how they wished (allowed to play with them). The latter group had more perseverance at the task and were inventive in their strategies to solve that problem. One could say that the first group were the 'know that' group and the second were the 'know how' group.

It would be simplistic to suggest that all new learning needs to be based on first-hand experience. However, it would appear that young children in particular need to be able to associate new knowledge within a context that makes sense to them, and that a notion of knowledge for knowledge's sake, disassociated from a meaningful relevance, is unlikely to engage a young child's curiosity and maintain their interest. The decontextualised questions that we have become so used to asking children as part of our assessment processes make very little sense to them and are therefore likely to elicit only a tepid response.

In an era when the word 'play' seems permanently wedded to the word 'station', it continues to be difficult to conceive of the idea of play being a useful method of learning new knowledge in educational settings. Play is seen as frivolous, inconsequential and certainly not educationally sound. In their work on teachers teaching playfully, Bennett *et al.* (1997) found that early years teachers were very clear that children should be learning through play but that 'the commitment to a play-based curriculum, a central tenet of the ideological tradition, appears to be based on rhetoric rather than on sound pedagogical reasoning'. If early years teachers themselves are anxious and unclear as to how to teach playfully, how can parents and non-specialists be confident that these young children are learning effectively through this nebulous method? Insecurity and lack of pedagogical leadership has led to a culture of inarticulacy which, in itself, has often tempted teachers down the 'work, before play' road.

Play versus work

Apart from the muddled thinking that underpins a 'work, before play' approach, practitioners we have talked to find this an unsatisfactory method for the following reasons:

- Children do not concentrate on their work because they are rushing to finish so that they can play.
- Working children are distracted by playing children.
- There is no way to divide the workers from the players in the space available.
- The play is often of poor quality as there is no adult available to supervise the play; they are all engaged with the working children.

Two get engrossed at a deeper level

This, then, becomes a self-fulfilling prophecy. A setting which has work as the higher-profile activity ensures that most of the resources and adult presence will be concentrated around these 'more important' activities, which are probably reading, writing or learning to count in adult-led activities in a formal context. The play provision will, most likely, be less well attended by staff, not planned so thoroughly and possibly not used to assess children's progress. Poor behaviour is likely to follow, as the area used for play is uninviting and cramped, reinforcing the view that the play is nothing more than playing about.

The worry is that despite the introduction of the *Curriculum Guidance for the Foundation Stage* which unequivocally states that 'well-planned play . . . is a key way children learn with enjoyment and challenge', recent research (ATL 2004), found that

opportunities for high-quality learning experiences for the children were few and far between.

Overall we observed few opportunities for

- Sustained, shared purposeful talk
- Sustained, complex imaginative play
- Authentic and engaging first-hand experiences.

One of the main reasons the researchers found for this implementation gap between theory and practice was that 'While most LEA advisers stated that understanding pedagogy and child development were vital topics for training, less than a fifth of other respondents, including teachers, rated them highly'. Most practitioners seem to be influenced more by their own experiences, schemes of work, school policies and school ethos, rather than by principles of good practice. While acknowledging that engaged, purposeful children learned well, few seemed able to link this to play in their settings.

To try to untangle the misconceptions about play, it may be helpful to consider the positive attributes of play and then to consider the practical consequences of adopting play as a means of teaching. These would seem to be as follows:

- Perhaps most importantly, the most obvious quality that play has is that children clearly enjoy it. If children consistently find the business of learning new knowledge and skills an exciting one and develop positive dispositions towards new learning they are likely to become 'masterful' and competent learners.

- The process of play allows children to engage with learning actively, interactively and independently, both in body and mind. This, as we discussed in Chapter 1, accords with how children learn most effectively and it would seem sensible to teach children in ways in which they can access new knowledge most successfully. Play can be solitary or co-operative and always affords a level of autonomy to the child.

- Play provides the child with the opportunity to think creatively, to enter alternative worlds and to confront challenging issues in a safe environment. Children can play at being in hospital, coping with a new sibling, as well as practising adult roles by driving trains, boiling kettles and building space stations; anything is possible! It is by developing the thinking skills that accompany these activities that children begin to learn how to solve problems, think laterally and work collaboratively.

- Play allows a child to join an activity at a level that is developmentally appropriate for them as individuals. A workshop area in the setting will provide stimulation for the child who is building on previous experience of constructing a bird with moving wings as well as for the child who is new to the mysteries of the Sellotape dispenser.

- Perhaps the most problematic attribute of play from the practitioner's point of view is that it places the child firmly in control of the process. From the point of view of the learning child, this is a positive attribute as they are able to learn what *they* need to know (as opposed to what the practitioner wants them to know) in ways that are effective. However, for the adults in the setting, there are huge difficulties in what is often seen as 'handing over control' to very young children, particularly as the responsibility for ensuring successful learning remains with the adults.

Bennett *et al.* (1997) characterised teachers' contrasting views of work and play as bipolar constructs at opposite ends of a continuum. Table 2.1 shows how teachers in their research described work and play.

Table 2.1 Play–work bipolar constructs

Play is usually thought of as:	Work is often thought of as:
Enjoyable	Onerous
Child-initiated	Teacher-initiated
Child-directed	Teacher-directed
Independent	Dependent
Children know what they need	Teachers know what they need
Appropriate	Sometimes inappropriate
Incidental	Planned
Unplanned developments	Intended learning outcomes
Active learning mode	Passive learning mode
Collaborative teacher role	Didactic teacher role
Informal assessment	Formal assessment
Socio-affective outcomes	Cognitive outcomes

The following example will highlight the confused thinking around play and work. In one nursery, a four-year-old boy stated that he preferred attending his nursery to the playgroup he used to go to because at the playgroup he had had to do 'real work' whereas at nursery he could play. When questioned a little further it became clear that his 'work' had consisted of paper and pencil exercises and that it was because of their inappropriateness that he had disliked them. He did, in fact, recognise that he did 'difficult' things at nursery but because he enjoyed them he had categorised them as 'play', which his parents then interpreted as time-wasting. Added to this, his parents believed that formal learning such as worksheet activities were appropriate for him and commented that 'I never found learning easy so I expect he is just the same'. They clearly felt that if their son found these activities hard he should do more of them, and expressed the commonly held view that if the activities were proving to be difficult this was proof of their effectiveness.

What can I do with it?

It is easy to see how such a polarised view of ways of learning can confuse the new practitioner who may have considered the theories of active, interactive and independent learning during training but finds that in practice a more formal regime is in place.

Play as a process

Further complications arise when trying to categorise or define play as an activity. Terms such as 'structured' are often thought to raise the standard of playing to validate it within the educational setting and to reassure anxious parents. Without a framework by a trained adult it is thought that play may be very successful at engaging children's hands but not so successful at engaging their brains. In support of this view, research conducted in the 1980s by Sylva in Oxford found that play in settings was a low-level activity which lacked cognitive challenge. Kenneth Baker, as education minister in the 1980s, famously remarked that he was determined to end 'all this cutting and sticking in the nursery'. The conundrum here, however, is that once adults take a controlling role in play by determining the outcome ('a picture to take home for Mummy') or the time-frame ('finish quickly now, it's nearly snack time') or the use of resources ('we don't do paint mixing till the Reception class'), what the children are doing is less likely to be high quality play and may be in danger of ceasing to be play altogether.

Better, perhaps, to think of play 'as a process and not in terms of its content' (Moyles 1994). When play is of poor quality in settings, it would appear to be either because of a lack of understanding on the part of the practitioners or because of a lack of conviction in the process. Both of these difficulties can be addressed by considering play as a *process of learning* rather than a *type of activity*. A way in to this line of thought may be to make comparisons with play in adults.

A consideration of adults at play, or engaging in their hobbies, usually finds their enthusiasm linked to a range of attributes that are similar to the things children enjoy about their play. Hobbies are self-chosen, with the participant deciding whether to be part of a group or alone. Often a hobby can be both, with, say, a gardener being happy with their own company in their garden yet equally keen to share ideas and produce at a garden club. Progress is often made through pitting oneself against past achievements or, in team games, training hard in the support of the team's performance. Being in control and being able to take independent decisions about the level of commitment leads to pleasure and enjoyment. Stress tends to be positive as it is self-measured and therefore is at a level that appears manageable. A glance at Table 2.1 shows that the attributes of adults' hobbies are clearly of the 'play' variety and yet most adults would claim to put every effort into their hobbies, to engage fully with them and to achieve highly as a result. Perhaps there are aspects of the adult's playful processes that practitioners would do well to harness in order to help children achieve highly.

Conversely, there may well be aspects of work that are enjoyable and have a playful feel to them. Adults' places of work may offer stimulation and challenge, a rich exchange of ideas with like-minded colleagues and opportunities to extend their skills and abilities. The more closely one considers the work–play divide, the more blurred the edges become. The resulting process which one might call playful learning, or serious playfulness, does seem to link happily with current brain research. This suggests that it is by engaging in these rather looser, less goal-orientated processes that children are interested and motivated. Synapse production is optimised and the repetition and the practice that play provide aid synapse stabilisation in the immature brain, leading towards a sound understanding of concepts.

Play and the brain

Brain studies exploring the functioning of neurones and relatively new areas of study such as cognitive science are giving us new ways of looking at effective learning. The discipline of cognitive science, for example, as described by

Claxton (1997), suggests two layers of functioning of which only one, sometimes called 'intelligence', is currently valued in Western society. He argues that a second layer, or 'undermind', which is that part of our brain which is 'relaxed, leisurely and playful', is seriously undervalued. This has important implications for young children who are engaged with a content curriculum at school, assimilating large bodies of knowledge quickly with little consideration given to developing learning skills or time to consolidate what they have been taught. The 'undermind' is the part of the brain in which new ideas are considered, mulled over, and where the process of Piaget's theories of assimilation, accommodation and equilibration takes place. It is often a slow business and requires what Eric Jenson (1998) referred to as 'downtime'. This downtime, or processing time, allows new synapses, which are formed at the acquisition of new knowledge, time to strengthen. This can only happen with an absence of other stimuli competing with them. This idea raises interesting questions about children's ability to learn confidently in a society which prizes intellectual achievement in a 'Think fast, we need the results' culture. Claxton (1997) argues that in a state of continual urgency and harassment the mind's activity is channelled towards conventional responses even if they may be wrong. To encourage alternative solutions and new ideas the brain needs to be challenged but not anxious. A concentration on the 'mental maths approach', so prevalent in some Reception classes, could be very damaging to young learners' confidence and self-esteem. Certainly the link to creativity is clear. Whether the creator is a scientist, a writer, an artist or a gardener, a playful process of 'Let's try it this way' and 'I wonder what would happen if . . .' forms an integral part of discovering and making something new. The islands of competence and expertise that children build up through their play provide them with secure areas of understanding from which to launch themselves into the sea of new knowledge which is waiting to be discovered by the confident learner.

Children's schematic play

Children's innate learning strategies help them on this journey of discovery. Cathy Nutbrown (1994), in her work on children's schematic play, talks of children's 'forms of thought or patterns of behaviour that have threads of thinking running through them'. These threads of thinking, when supported by attuned adults, will consolidate into securely understood concepts and knowledge. This definition has as its basis one of Piaget's most firmly grounded assumptions, that is, that the child is an active participant in the development of knowledge and thereby constructs its own understanding. In so constructing, Piaget believed that children try to adapt to the world around them, making ever more sense of their surroundings as they do so. His ideas concerning the basic processes of gaining new understanding, those of assimilation, accommodation and equilibration, are clearly observable in schematic play.

The theory of schematic play is that confident children and adults think in their heads, but if we are less confident about something, we keep track of our thoughts by using something to represent them externally. Adults may use shopping lists, maps, diagrams or gestures to keep hold of otherwise slippery ideas, or we may think through and practise an important conversation, such as an interview, to remind ourselves of those aspects which are important to us. Very young children are still developing their thinking skills and so need to do this most of the time.

Their schemas show what they are learning; we can see it happening and watch them thinking. Schemas in young children are thought to concern basic concepts such direction (up and down, core and radial, concentric), transport (here to there), connection (joining), enclosure (inside, outside, wrapping), covering (layering) and trajection (fast, straight lines). Competence in vertical and horizontal schemas translate later into skills such as letter formation, block graphs, crosswords and bus timetables. Schemas are also thought not only to encompass a three-dimensional aspect to learning but also to help with the concept of time in giving children opportunities to learn about sequence, and, consequently, cause and effect. In general, schemas can be said to encompass ideas and actions that are shaping a child's current learning interests.

An example of a piece of schematic play recently seen in a nursery class was that of Joanne and Jenny, who carefully and efficiently emptied the home corner by packing up the entire contents into bags and hooking them onto the babies' buggies. The buggies were then wheeled to a different area in the setting, the bathroom, which was quite unsuitable as a home play area. All the bags were unpacked and the contents painstakingly laid out to provide a sumptuous picnic! When questioned by a puzzled adult, the girls replied that they would put it all back 'very soon' but were unable to give a rational explanation for their actions. This is probably because they had no logical explanation but were subject to a compulsive play pattern which was helping them to learn about transporting, in other words, how things get from one place to another.

Once adults have some knowledge of schematic play patterns, many other instances of repeated play behaviour begin to come to mind. One such is the train track which stretches from one side of the setting to the other but rarely sees a train! This may well be because this schema involves learning about how objects join together but is not concerned with how the train runs along the track. Giving children a workshop with materials to join together using a range of methods, such as glue, Sellotape and staples, gives those investigating the joining schema opportunities to satisfy their need to experiment and become proficient. Schemas tend to be tightly specific and compulsively repeated, often in different ways, which helps concepts to be securely learned or multi-embodied. A child concerned with circles may draw and paint them and dance them and enjoy making round cakes, gaining more competence and understanding of the concept with each experience. A child learning about the trajectory schema may need to have their learning supported so that there is not too much disruption with fingers placed under taps of running water! Woodwork helps here, as does the opportunity to kick balls and play basketball and jump. Interestingly, children who investigate a schema in great depth cannot easily be persuaded to widen their interests. They will progress to a level of considerable competence but will usually only excel in one area. This means not that they will be incompetent in the development of other concepts but that they will normally not investigate others with the compulsion that they have shown for their chosen schema.

Supporting children's schematic play is satisfying not only because understanding what may appear to be irrational and often infuriating behaviour helps the practitioner's state of mind, but also because channelling the behaviour renders it manageable and profitable within the context of everyday learning experiences. Children who are encouraged in their schematic play will learn effectively and, as their thinking about their preferred concept develops, will be able to progress to more sophisticated levels of understanding until they have internalised the concept and no longer have need for external reminders. Adults will then notice that the schematic play stops and children will talk about, reflect on and demonstrate understanding of their new concept with certainty.

How to incorporate schemas into planning the provision

In the example above, Joanne and Jenny spent some days transporting the contents of the home corner to the bathroom. After a staff meeting it was suggested that they be encouraged to take it into the garden to minimise disruption but still encourage the transporting to be experienced. Then, the musical instruments went outside and then were brought back again and, in due course, Joanne and Jenny became the children who took the register to the general office and messages to other teachers in the school. It was suggested that this interest could usefully be widened into a half term's project entitled 'From Here to There'. This was duly put into place and it provided many rich opportunities for travelling to and fro. During the exploration of this topic the children worked through various aspects of movement such as categorising things that move and things that don't, how to make things move, the direction of movement, different types of movement and the effects of movement. Children's thinking skills were developed through searching questions such as 'What moves?', 'Do things move on their own or do we need to make them move?' and 'How do we do that?'

One of the most exciting pieces of learning to emerge from this project came from Jenny's observation that, of course, messages move from one place to another. She had experienced this while taking messages around the school. To progress this idea the staff began writing postcards to the nursery address, and it was not long before children were posting cards to their friends at nursery (and sometimes to themselves!). They would wait impatiently for the postman to deliver them each day. He responded by inviting the staff and children to the local sorting office, which itself provided a rich stimulus for real-life learning. This project incorporated all the required curriculum areas of learning in practical, interesting ways and allowed each child to engage with an aspect of it at an appropriate level. The planning provided for a depth of study so that children would not lose interest; they made toys with simple wind-up mechanisms and some furthered their interest in circulatory schemas by investigating objects that turned (mincers, spinning tops, windmills, whisks, clocks). It also provided for a breadth of study so that all the children could find, within the parameters of the topic, enough to arouse their curiosity and encourage their positive dispositions to learn. There was some recording of, for example, which boat won the race across the water tray and which came second and third but on the whole this was learning by doing and the only recording was integral and necessary.

This project was an example of playful learning where children can be seen to be displaying some of the dimensions ascribed to work, such as struggle, persistence, collaboration and the ability to solve problems.

Play and active learning

This type of playful learning is effective because it is active, interactive and encourages independence. It might be useful to consider how to provide for it in practice. It is a truism that a practitioner's beliefs are evidenced by the appearance of the setting. Put simply, if the teacher or manager believes that children learn through active engagement with the planned environment there will be:

- a place for groups to meet, to read, sing and dance together;
- an area for construction to encourage building and imaginative small-world play;
- a role-play area where children can engage in symbolic play;
- a graphics area for trying out a range of drawing and writing activities;
- interactive displays which may have been started by an adult but can be added to or changed by children – here children may add words to

a well-known story or use small-world people and animals to act out their version of rhymes and stories;

- sand and water play, as extensive as possible;
- an area for painting and printing including colour mixing and a choice of paper and brush sizes;
- a place to listen to story tapes and read books;
- somewhere to play musical instruments, a range of pitched and unpitched instruments;
- display boards at child height for children to attach their own pictures and messages;
- a workshop for learning the skills of design technology.

There will not be a table and chair for every child to sit down at the same time, there is unlikely to be a teacher's desk and parents/carers will feel welcome when they enter the setting.

Remembering the debate in Chapter 1 about the difference between 'activities' and 'provision', it can be seen from this list that the setting based on first-hand experiences relies more heavily on *provision*, which can be used flexibly to support child-initiated learning, rather than on *activities* which rely on a fixed adult input and agenda.

Active learners in this type of setting will find:

- first-hand experiences which are meaningful and relevant and worthy of active engagement;
- activities and experiences which cause them to ask questions rather than answer adults' closed questions;
- a variety of ways to follow up what has aroused their curiosity and intrigued them;
- a degree of autonomy in how they explore and investigate the provision;
- resources that are of good quality which can be used flexibly to suit the learner's purpose.

Genuinely active learning involves the possibility that what is learned is as flexible as the resources that have been provided. Spontaneous learning is a sign that the setting is rich in these possibilities but it is impossible to plan for, which sometimes causes anxiety in today's climate of 'structured' play. Structure is present in the flexible setting as all the provision has been planned and has worthwhile educational content. This means that both the children and the adults have confidence that spontaneous learning will be every bit as valuable as adult-initiated learning.

Play and unexpected learning

Max, for example, found something 'black and round and slimy' in an old sink in the garden one day in early spring. On further investigation and after much heated debate with an adult, it was decided that this was frogspawn. No adult can plan for the arrival of frogspawn but the staff had remembered that it was about this time last year that it had arrived and so had checked out the picture books, charcoal, drawing paper and magnifying glasses in anticipation of a repeat visit! The initial learning was, of necessity, unplanned but was later incorporated into the following week's schedule.

To support children in becoming interactive learners there need to be opportunities for them to talk through their understandings, problems and ideas with a friend or an adult. They need an environment where language use is valued both as a means of communication and as fun. Jimmy, who was playing with the water outside, had spilled some onto the ground which was flowing towards a drain. The practitioner lifted up the drain cover because the children wanted to know where the water went next. Jimmy stood, peering down into the drain and said:

> 'Baa, baa, black sheep have you any wool?
> Yes, sir, yes sir, three bags full,
> One for the master and one for the dame
> And one for the little boy who lives down the drain.'

An environment that uses provision flexibly, takes advantage of the unexpected and encourages questioning is one that provides the opportunity for creative thinking and invention. Perhaps Jimmy would talk through his idea of a boy living down the drain with an adult and decide to make up a story, paint a picture or just take pleasure in his new-found ability to understand the concept of rhymes. The outcome is less important than the fact that the setting in which he is being educated provides him with an environment where he is developing positive dispositions towards learning and that he has access to both adults and children with whom to share his experiences.

Play and interactions

The genuinely interactive setting will have as one of its core principles the understanding that talk is a key process of learning. The principle that learning is a social process and that spoken language is integral to successful learning have been explored by Lev Vygotsky (1986) and are further examined in Chapter 5.

It is important to consider the nature of interactivity and its link to playful behaviours. Early interactivity has its roots in the home. Bruner and Sherwood (1975), in their essay on the beginnings of interactivity, describe the conventions of the game, Peek-a-Boo, where children experiment and then refine the concepts of disappearance and reappearance, of turn-taking and of experimenting with language. The reciprocity of this near-universal activity observed in babies and toddlers seems to suggest that it is rich in the range of learning opportunities it offers. Apart from the physical movement and the added 'Boo', there is huge enjoyment expressed by both players and the chance for either player to initiate the game, which babies were seen to do after 12 months of age. It tackles the challenge of object permanence in a safe, playful way which requires reciprocal trust in both parties. The emotional commitment to the game is significant, emphasising once again the importance of resilience and confidence in the successful learning of new ideas. Games which encourage interactivity are still much enjoyed in early years settings, where they emphasise turn-taking and speaking and listening as a precursor to developing conversation skills. It is helpful to understand the components of speaking and listening when planning activities and provision.

Listening is about:

- obtaining information, instructions and directions;
- responding to and reflecting on others' ideas, experiences and opinions;
- establishing relationships, interacting and appreciating the feelings of others;
- gaining creative and aesthetic pleasure.

Talking is about:

- conveying information, instructions and directions;
- establishing relationships, interacting and expressing feelings;
- representing, sharing, clarifying and reflecting on ideas, experiences and opinions;
- giving and gaining imaginative and aesthetic pleasure.

Giving children genuine opportunities to be together in pairs and groups both with and without an adult, and giving them interesting things to talk and think about, will be hard to achieve in an environment which is predominantly adult led and where adults do not value what children have to say. Recently, we have heard Year 2 teachers say that children in their class can write clearly, accurately and neatly but can think of nothing to write about. This may be a result of three years of schooling where interactivity has been limited and the children have not been able to use complex spoken language spontaneously for a range of purposes.

Interactivity can be encouraged if the setting is managed to support it. Areas that are physically arranged in corners to invite children in for long periods of time will enable them to commit time to what is on offer and to get engrossed at a deep level. Areas that encourage children to rush past, with barely a glance at the provision, result in less commitment and a shallower level of engagement. An example of this was the interactive display of things that move, set up as part of the 'From Here to There' project. Three rectangular tables, arranged in a 'U' shape, invited children into the area. Once inside the 'U' there were interesting machines and toys to play with and talk about. There were colourful pictures and a bank of descriptive words to support children who were able to define movement in terms of 'spinning', 'swinging', 'rolling', 'bouncing', 'hopping', 'gliding' and so on.

The area was designed so that children could gain from it at a range of levels. Those new to the idea of considering movement as a concept could use the equipment and try out the accompanying spoken language while others could try making windmills in the workshop or boats in the water tray. Jerome Bruner called this a 'play spiral' and suggested that children, through play, would increase their understanding of a concept and gain mastery of it by a process of revision and practice. This is mirrored in the adult world if one thinks of evening classes, which are often structured into 'beginners', 'intermediate' and 'experienced', giving participants the opportunity to self-select as appropriate. An integral dimension of a rich play activity is one which provides for a range of learning opportunities, from watching what is happening, through joining in, to taking responsibility for using the play creatively.

Play and progression

Children's progression through playful learning, from observer to responsible innovator, is well provided for in these looser themes such as 'From Here to There'. The variety and flexibility of ideas feed children's imaginations far more than the more restrictive themes sometimes seen in settings. 'People who help us' is a standard topic which is often repeated and well catered for by commercial companies in terms of resources. However, it tends to be one-dimensional and predictable and so practitioners find it difficult to excite children's interest in probing deeper and more broadly into the learning possibilities the topic offers.

Richer themes will cater well for the exploratory, representational and free-flow play which Tina Bruce defined (1987) and which is so clearly seen in children's enthusiastic responses to genuinely interesting activities and provision. Children engaged in exploratory play will be asking themselves the question 'What is this and what does it do?' Those who have explored a new concept will be ready to begin to take control of it by 'representing' it or practising using it for their own purposes. Their question will be 'What can I do with it?' A child who has practised a concept or skill that they are mastering may be said to have reached a level of competency which allows them to bring to their play all that they have experienced in terms of knowledge, skills and feelings.

These are then integrated into their play, which is often called 'free-flow play'; this is play of which children take control, often inventing a plot and characters or perhaps designing an object, a dance or a painting. It is this type of play that encourages children to ask the question 'What if . . .?' and requires them to use their creative and imaginative skills. Children operating at this level can be said to be learning effectively as they are talking to each other, listening to others' ideas, experimenting, persevering with difficulties and solving problems. Carr *et al.* (2000), in their work on evaluating early childhood programmes using the New Zealand early years framework, described children's observable behaviours as they progressed from 'taking an interest', through 'being involved', 'persisting with difficulty', 'expressing a view or feeling' to 'taking responsibility'. It could be argued that having reached the stage of 'taking an interest', no progression beyond that level is possible without interaction with both the provision and with other children. The learning dispositions that Carr *et al.* ascribe to the business of interacting with learning, those of courage and curiosity, trust and playfulness, perseverance, confidence and taking responsibility, would appear to be universal, as they apply to learning in settings in just the same way as they do to the 'Peek-a-Boo' game in babies.

Interactivity, as we have suggested, requires the setting to be physically arranged so that children can engage actively with each other. It also requires a culture that trusts children, believes in their abilities to have some control over the ways in which they learn, and which values and gives time to listen to what they have to say. The system of 'plan, do, review', which grew out of the Headstart project in America, gives children just these opportunities to be interactive as they plan with an adult, responsibly carry out their chosen tasks and then reflect on their success to a small group. If these small-group times are discussions in which children's agendas are followed and their concerns and interests are paramount, children will grow in the confidence and self-esteem they need to initiate and be innovative and creative in their learning.

Adults who are partners in this adventure need, of course, to have a deep understanding of, and belief in, the principles of active and interactive practice, and we will look in some depth at the role of the reflective practitioner in the chapter on independent learning, Chapter 8.

Conclusion

It is hoped that a case has been made for a type of high level active and interactive learning which, by being playful, takes the learning to the child rather than expecting the child to come to the learning. It reflects a powerful model of what Bruner called 'learning how' and gives children not knowledge for knowledge's sake but a set of strategies that can be applied to successfully learning new knowledge throughout life.

POINTS FOR REFLECTION

Yourself

Consider how you think of play. Is it an alternative to the serious business of work or a process through which children can learn more effectively?

Your practice

Good organisation is one of the keys to effective play. Observe the team in your setting with regard to how they enable play as an effective learning mechanism.

References

Association of Teachers and Lecturers (ATL) (2004) *Inside the Foundation Stage: Recreating the Reception Year.* London: ATL.

Bennett, N., Wood, L. and Rogers, S. (1997) *Teaching Through Play.* Buckingham: Open University Press.

Bruce, T. (1987) *Early Childhood Education.* Sevenoaks: Hodder and Stoughton.

Bruner, J. (1976) 'Nature and uses of immaturity', in J. Bruner, A. Jolly and K. Sylva (eds) *Play: Its Role in Development and Evolution.* New York: Basic Books.

Bruner, J. and Sherwood, V. (1975) 'Peek-a-boo and the learning of rule structures', in J. Bruner, A. Jolly and K. Sylva (eds) *Play: Its Role in Development and Evolution* (pp. 277–85). Harmondsworth: Penguin Books.

Bruner, J., Sylva, K. and Genova, P. (1976) 'The role of play in the problem solving of children 3–5 years old', in P. Barnes, J. Oates, J. Chapman, V. Lee and P. Czerniewska (eds) *Personality, Development and Learning.* Sevenoaks: Hodder and Stoughton.

Carr, M., May, H., Podmore, V., Cubey, P., Hatherly, A. and Macartney, B. (2000) *Learning and Teaching Stories: Action Research on Evaluation in Early Childhood. Final Report to the Ministry of Education.* Wellington: New Zealand Council for Educational Research.

Claxton, G. (1997) *Hare Brain, Tortoise Mind.* London: Fourth Estate.

Jenson, E. (1998) 'The brains behind the brain', *Journal of Education Leadership,* 56 (3), 20.

Moyles, J. (1994) *The Excellence of Play.* Buckingham: Open University Press.

Nutbrown, C. (1994) *Threads of Thinking.* London: Paul Chapman Publishing.

Vygotsky, L.S. (1986) *Thought and Language.* Cambridge, Mass: MIT Press.

CHAPTER 3

The world around

- Young children learn from everything that happens to them and around them.

- Curriculum interpretation depends on beliefs and principles. Ensure that learning builds on previous experiences.

Making sense of the world

Anyone who has experience of preschool children, either as parent, carer or teacher, will appreciate that children from birth onwards are trying to make sense of their world, to understand why and how things happen. Young children learn by trying to make sense of their experiences all the time. Their senses are often bombarded by exciting and even surprising new experiences and they have to integrate this new knowledge or information with what they already know. Their engagement with learning is holistic and is not compartmentalised by subject. Learning happens not only within the preschool setting but also within the wider world in which they are involved.

Take a brother and sister, for example, cooking a cake with their mother. Which area of learning are they engaged in? Mathematics, one might argue, as the ingredients have to be weighed and put together in a particular sequence. Or is it science? Combining materials and watching change; deciding whether it is reversible or not and using the senses of touch and smell to develop a conceptual understanding of the attributes of the ingredients. Or is it language? After all, you have discussed who the cake will be for and you have used mathematical and scientific language. Or maybe this activity is more to do with socialisation, turn-taking, negotiation and patience. The possibilities are endless and most would agree that no one area could be cited above another. In fact the integration of these areas of learning into one single task gives them a context with which the children can identify and demonstrates for them at the same time the uses and purposes of mathematics, science and language, and the need for appropriate social skills.

Contrary to this integrated approach, it is traditional within the UK school and preschool curricula to define children's learning by dividing it into subject areas such as mathematics, language and knowledge and understanding of the world. Sometimes this presentation of the curriculum is interpreted by practitioners as a body of knowledge that children must be taught directly, often in a didactic manner. It is clear, however, that young children do not see their own learning in this way and therefore these divisions are somewhat arbitrary.

In this chapter we will look at what is meant by 'curriculum' and explore ways in which the early years practitioner might approach the given curriculum. We also look at how practitioners might take into account children's outside school experiences, both giving this the status it deserves and using this wider understanding to contextualise new ideas.

What is meant by 'curriculum'?

Encarta World English Dictionary defines curriculum as 'the subjects taught at an educational institution, or the elements taught in a particular subject'. This is a simplistic definition and perhaps a more appropriate definition, particularly for the early years, would be the one that is used by Glenda Macnaughton, who sees the early childhood curriculum as a 'politically engaged process in which the educators' intentions and the children's involvement interact to produce the lived curriculum of a specific service' (Macnaughton 2003). This describes the early years curriculum as a course of action that is carried out for reasons that best serve the desired outcome of providing the children with what they need in terms of their education and, in the case of the early years, their care.

If this definition is to be believed, then the curriculum that can be found within any early years setting will not be merely confined to the guidelines and requirements of an externally imposed curriculum such as the English National Curriculum or Foundation Stage curriculum guidance but will also be dependent upon the beliefs and values of the practitioners within the setting. So a child taking part in a cooking activity will not only be learning the processes and skills and knowledge involved in making, for example, a birthday cake but will probably also learn, not least by the attitude of the adult, about the purposes of food in general and the importance of the cake as a symbol of a celebration.

We can find the building blocks of the early years curriculum for England in the *Curriculum Guidance for the Foundation Stage*. This sets out the expected outcomes in terms of knowledge, skills and concepts, of children's early education.

Learning best through hands-on experience

These outcomes give us the content to be learned. They match the knowledge, skills and understandings that are given high status within our society, such as being able to count and to read.

The written curriculum is just the beginning, the bare bones, which undergoes a metamorphosis as teachers and pupils interpret, modify and add to the meanings that it embodies (Alexander 2000). In this way the written curriculum is interpreted by practitioners and transformed by them into intended learning outcomes for learning tasks and activities or sensitive interactions during child-initiated play.

One of the ways in which this transformation might manifest itself in practice is shown in the following example of some children engaged in self-initiated play. Ben and Amy were playing in the play house. They had decided to engage in some pretend cooking. The practitioner, having a good understanding of the children's previous learning, encouraged the children to write down (in their own writing) the ingredients that they were using. In this way the practitioner had taken a learning goal from the Foundation Stage Curriculum and transformed it into a learning opportunity suitable for the children, in line with her own beliefs that children should learn through play in a context chosen by the children.

Baking cakes

The curriculum transformation that comes about in any setting will depend on the beliefs and values of the setting as a whole and individuals within that setting. This is because the ways in which staff choose to interact with the children and with each other, the social and cultural values they bring to the setting and the way in which they structure learning experiences will affect the outcome for the children (Lubeck 1985; Hartley 1993), and children will develop, for example, attitudes to the processes of learning and teaching dependent on staff attitude. If the staff, for example, listen to and respect each other's opinions, the children will in turn develop a respect for each other. They will be more prepared to listen to others and feel more confident to contribute to discussion as they will understand, through the example set by the adults, that their ideas will be valued.

The skills, concepts and different understandings that children develop will also depend on the 'invisible pedagogy' being used within their setting. A child who has learned to count by counting out the number of chairs needed for the teddies in the play house or counting out the number of drinks needed for all the children in the session, for example, will have a different understanding of the uses of counting from the child who has learned to count objects set out by the practitioner for no obvious purpose other than practising the mechanics of counting.

It is clear, then, that although all practitioners may be working from the same curriculum document, the actual curriculum that is presented to the children, while similar in content, may be very different in process and in the attitudes and dispositions to learning that will develop in the children. The important thing to do, when trying to understand the curriculum that you are presenting or wish to present within your setting, is to examine your own beliefs about how children learn, your own cultural values and what you consider are the purposes of education, as this will give you a valuable insight into the 'hidden curriculum' that you are presenting.

Understanding how children learn and its importance for developing a curriculum

The development of suitable curricula for our youngest children is dependent on us having a good understanding of our own values and beliefs concerning the ways in which their education should be conducted. In turn, the development of values and beliefs can only be achieved by a secure understanding of how young children learn. Such understanding underpins the work of many early years practitioners in England. For many practitioners there is a sense that:

> each child comes to a preschool setting with unique experiences from family, home and community; that childhood should be a time of spontaneity and of exploration according to individual interests; and that didactic, teacher planned instruction has no part in an early years teacher's repertoire – is in fact a waste of time – because children learn best through 'hands on' self chosen play experiences.
>
> (David 2001: 55)

Ideas that see early learning as grounded in children's activities, socially constructed and context driven and that place the child as central to his or her own learning have not just come about by ad hoc experiences or anecdotal reporting. Indeed the weight of research, as has already been discussed in previous chapters, suggests that the acquisition of knowledge and understanding stems not only from exploration but also from mediated social practice (Bruner 1983; Rogoff 1990) and communication. In addition Vygotsky believed that it is important for young children to have the support of others if they are to learn. Children develop their knowledge most effectively in contexts that they can understand and it is clear that preschool children need to be suitably stimulated by a curriculum which allows them to connect the unknown to the known and thus to assimilate understanding.

A term that has been used by some researchers to describe this mediated but active role for the learner is that of 'apprenticeship' (Bruner 1983; Rogoff 1990). Rogoff believes that this term describes the way in which children learn effectively within shared problem solving; where both the learner and the more experienced other participate in 'culturally organised activity' (Rogoff 1990).

Being sensitively proactive in helping the children to develop their understanding of a task they are engaged in is important, as it is clear that practitioners taking a passive role, so that children learn only through play, may not release all the potential that children have for learning. At the same time, direct instruction models can be counterproductive and pedagogical practices that embody too much control over children's choices, their play and discovery may not be beneficial in the longer term (Meade 1999). Therefore a model that falls somewhere between these two extremes seems to be the most appropriate.

The following extract is taken from an observation in a playgroup. Take a look at the extract and try to identify what the role of the practitioner is here. Think about her use of direct instructions, where her practice might be described as supportive, where she allows some autonomy for the child and whether there is an element of choice and play.

James asks to join in a cooking activity and the practitioner agrees that he can.
PRACTITIONER: What should you do before you cook, James?
James goes to wash his hands, puts on an apron and returns to the table.
PRACTITIONER: Let me just check your hands to make sure they are clean, please, (*looks at hands*) that's fine, well done.
PRACTITIONER: Now we need 200 grams of butter. What can we use to get it out of the tub?
JAMES: The spoon.
He chooses a metal spoon and offers it to the practitioner. The practitioner offers James the tub of butter so that he can put spoonfuls onto the scales. She helps the children weigh out the ingredients to make biscuit mixture and the children knead the dough using their hands. The practitioner then helps them to roll out some of the mixture each. She picks up a heart cutter and shows the children how to use it.
PRACTITIONER: It is best to do hearts for the first ones because they take a longer time to cook than the others.
Children follow the adult's lead and choose a heart cutter The practitioner demonstrates to the children on her own biscuit mix.
PRACTITIONER: Don't go over the edge, careful, look.
She helps James to move cutter into a space.
JAMES: Why do we have to do heart shapes first?
PRACTITIONER: Because they take different times to cook. We will put the hearts in the oven first and then we can do some other shapes.
Children cut the heart shapes and the practitioner helps them to put them on the baking tray and then into the oven. They then choose from the other shapes to make more biscuits. Later the children are able to eat the biscuits that they have made.

(Observation 4:6; Bottle 2003)

The views we have explored in this section, which are based on theories of child development, are not, as might be assumed, at odds with the government guidelines for children in their early years. In fact the Qualifications and Curriculum

Authority (QCA) define the curriculum as 'everything the children do, see, hear or feel in their setting both planned and unplanned' (QCA 2000: 1) and indeed the given intention of the Foundation Stage guidance is not that areas of learning and subjects should be taught in isolation. This is because, although our historical roots in an elementary or social imperatives egalitarian model of curriculum mean that we continue to present literacy and numeracy skills as a priority, there is also a recognition that play is an important vehicle for learning. Furthermore, the Foundation Stage curriculum guidance takes into account, through the 'Stepping Stones', that each child is an individual with unique previous experiences.

What do children do at home?

It is recognised by most early years practitioners that children arrive at the preschool setting with a variety of experiences and that it is important for curriculum development that practitioners have a sense of what has gone before in order to plan effectively for each child's development.

Learning at home is a socially constructed activity with parents, children and siblings interacting together, often engaging in a considerable complexity and diversity of activity. The types of activities that children engage in at home will vary from family to family. Some children, for example, help with household tasks such as supermarket shopping and baking. Some have had experience of card or board games (Saxe *et al.* 1987; Tizard and Hughes 1984; Bottle 2003). They may also play with bricks and construction kits as well as other toys, both large such as bikes and dolls' prams, and small such as miniature worlds. Some will also have access to books and, increasingly, to computer games.

Children's learning at home is rarely compartmentalised and different concepts such as shape, space and measures, for example, are learned together (Nutbrown 1994). In addition, children engage in activity more effectively and their concentration spans increase when they have a personal interest in the activity. Tim, for example, was playing at home with his mother. He had decided to build a bridge for his toy car to go underneath but found that his car was too tall to go through.

Tim builds a bridge with one piece of Duplo for each leg and a long piece of Duplo for the horizontal span. Tries to put his car under the bridge.
MUM: It won't go through it.
She picks up bridge and adds bricks to legs. Tim tries to help.
MUM: That's it, like this. *She shows Tim how to put the bricks together and builds a taller bridge.* Mum's going to make a toy bridge for your car. *She puts the bridge down on the carpet.* Ready, ready! *She pushes the car through the bridge. Tim picks up the bridge and removes one leg.*
MUM: Mummy's poor bridge.

(Observation, aged 20 months; Bottle 2003)

This is a short extract from the interaction that occurred between Tim and his mother in which they continued to make and remake the bridge, for about ten minutes, until they were both satisfied with the result. Even within the short piece given here you can see that Tim has a personal interest in the activity and that shape and space (the room needed under the bridge for the car to go through) is being learned alongside measure (how many bricks to make the bridge high enough).

It is thought that young children learn most effectively in contextualised situations (Donaldson 1978) and some children have the opportunity to experience activities which are firmly embedded in everyday contexts, such as household domestic activity or the child's self-initiated play. These types of activity allow for reflective observation and questioning. For example, Tim was making pretend tea:

MUM: Mummy could do with a cup of tea, please.
TIM: Do you want any sugar?
MUM: Two, please.
TIM: OK, but I've only got three.
MUM: Oh well, three will be fine!
TIM: *He pretends to put in three spoons of sugar.* 'One. Two. Three. It only had three but that's all right because I put three in yours.

(Observation, aged 4:6; Bottle 2003)

Through this type of contextualised activity some children are also given opportunities for active experimentation of the same concepts in different contexts. Tim's experiences of counting, for example, also appeared in a variety of other situations as Tim also counted trains, pictures in a book and pieces of paper chain, and practised the number sequence (Bottle 2003). A child who has had experiences rich in contextual versatility may develop a better understanding of the relationship between other areas of learning than a child who has not had this type of experience at home.

Many of the contextualised, non-compartmentalised activities that children experience at home are ad hoc and informal. Conversely some activities are undertaken with the probable intention by the parent of teaching, for example board games. Such activities, while often having concrete experiences associated with them, for example moving counters along a board, did not perhaps have the same opportunities for reflection and questioning as the less formal experiences. The following extract demonstrates how such activity can allow the child to learn specific concepts and shows how they may have a tendency to be compartmentalised, with little room for integration into other concept areas.

Lizzie and her mother are sitting on the floor, doing a puzzle.
MUM: Who's that?
LIZZIE: Annie Apple, Bouncy Ben.
MUM: There we are, then. Who might you need next?
LIZZIE: Clever Cat.

Mum looks through the pieces. Lizzie watches, then picks out Clever Cat.

MUM: There she is. Put Clever Cat in . . . Who might we need next?
Points to the space. Who comes here?

LIZZIE: Dippy Duck.

MUM: Got one, yes.

Lizzie puts Dippy duck in.

(Observation, aged 4:6; Bottle 2003).

We have already seen that the purpose of an activity and the type of interaction between parent and child can vary depending on the task. It is also the case though that the amount of interactions between parent and child at home can vary too. At one extreme there may be little or no participation or intervention from the parents and they can take a completely passive role towards the child's play. This passivity can lead to a lack of communication and a lack of challenge which according to Meade (1999) will not release the child's potential. At the other extreme there may be a great deal of participation or intervention but if this translates into an excessively controlling environment then it can also be detrimental. Meanwhile, the dangers of over-teaching on the parent's part could mean that the child may become anxious or unsure about using acquired knowledge. Children will bring these learned dispositions to the preschool setting with them.

Munn and Schaffer (1993) found the home environment to be relatively effective and highly adaptive to the child's cognitive functioning. Some parents, they found, are very good at being sensitive to their child's understanding and they are able to scaffold their child's emerging skills and understanding. An example of this sensitivity to the child's understanding can be seen in the following extract. Anna was playing a card game, which involved putting together an alien, with her grandmother when her mother intervened to help Grandma to set the task at the correct level for Anna:

GRAN: Eyes, put the eyes there, the feet on the bottom, he's got lots of hands, hasn't he?

ANNA: Hands.

GRAN: He's got lots of hands, how many hands has he got?

MUM: You had better start counting on with her, Mum. If you go, one, two . . .

GRAN: Look, how many hands, one . . .?

ANNA: Two.

GRAN: Three.

ANNA: Three, four.

GRAN: Four.

ANNA: Five, six.

(Observation, aged 2:2; Bottle 2003)

We can see, then, that there are large variations in young children's experiences within their home environment, and by the time children enter preschool they will have already developed a preferred learning style. Some children will be outgoing and lively, some quieter and more sedentary. Some will be interested and motivated and some will appear to do very little to further their own understanding independently. The preschool curriculum offered therefore needs to take into account not only the knowledge that they have before they enter preschool but also their attitudes and dispositions towards learning.

Identifying your own ideological stance

The word ideology has been defined by some educationalists as '. . . that system of beliefs which gives general direction to the educational policies of those who hold those beliefs' (Scrimshaw 1983) or as 'a set of ideas and beliefs which is often held by social groups who share particular interests' (Pollard 1996). Any particular ideology related to education can be described as a set of beliefs, values, ideas and opinions that shape the way an individual or a group of education practitioners thinks, acts and understands their field.

There are three main ideologies of education, which can be easily identified. These are not mutually exclusive and you may find that your personal beliefs, ideas, values and opinions fit into more than one of them.

The three main ideologies of education are:

1. the **child** is the prime concern of education;
2. gaining **knowledge** is the prime concern of education;
3. the needs of **society** are the prime concern of education.

Furthermore, some basic categories of primary school curriculum were identified by Robin Alexander (1988). These are listed below:

- **Classical Humanist** This type of curriculum ensures that the child is initiated into the best of their cultural heritage.
- **Behavioural/Mechanistic** This curriculum has observable and testable learning outcomes at progressively higher levels.
- **Elementary** The main aim of this type of curriculum is preparation for the workforce.
- **Social Imperatives** This category has two subcategories, which are an *adaptive* curriculum, which enables the children to meet the economic and social needs of society, or an *egalitarian*-based curriculum, which relies on the belief that all children should have equal opportunity and contribute to the progress of society.
- **Progressive** This type of curriculum is open and negotiable and expects the children to achieve their individual potential.

- **Developmental** This curriculum is underpinned by an understanding and knowledge of children's physiological and psychological development and learning.

The exploration of one's own ideas, beliefs and values leads to a recognition and understanding of one's own ideological stance. This is important because settings and practitioners will inevitably influence the children and ultimately society as we transmit our beliefs, ideas, opinions and values in everything we do or produce. Conversely, although all members of a group (for example, within your setting) will not hold the same values, beliefs, ideas and opinions, society will have an influence on these.

Look carefully at Alexander's categories and try to decide which of them matches most closely your own beliefs and values. In trying to tease out your own ideological stance, you may find that your beliefs and values fit in with more than one single ideological idea as given above. You will probably find though that your emphasis is in one area more than another and your values, ideas and beliefs will probably change over time. Sometimes there may be a mismatch between professed ideology and what happens in practice. This may be because we are not being honest about our beliefs and feel that an ideological stance that is not our own is more acceptable within the setting. Or it may be because outside pressures, such as inspection, give the impression that an alternative ideology to our own is preferred or even imposed. Knowledge of different ideologies may help us to acknowledge and deal with differing beliefs, ideas, values and opinions that we may encounter professionally.

Thinking about your own philosophy

Philosophies explain what we do and why we do it. They are the beliefs, principles or aims which underlie our practice or conduct. Deciding on what we will do with the children and how we will go about it may seem a practical matter but in reality our own philosophy of child education will influence the decisions that we make. What we believe will affect the way in which we decide to present any particular activity. Many early years practitioners have strong philosophical beliefs about the ways in which children learn but sometimes these beliefs are frustrated by what are perceived as the constraints of the Foundation Stage guidance, national initiatives such as the numeracy and literacy strategies, the National Curriculum and the inspection regime within which we are required to work.

Practitioners who are able to identify their own philosophy can look at the knowledge, skills and concepts content of the given curriculum and decide how best to ensure that the children achieve these goals, concentrating on the way experiences are created for the children and on how adults interact with each other and with the children. The focus can move from what the practitioner is teaching to what the children are learning and how that learning might take place. Turning the emphasis back on the child and their home experiences, developing skills, dispositions, needs and interests, and away from a curriculum or developmental area, allows the practitioner to look at the whole child and the whole learning experience.

If a practitioner has a clear philosophy, then curriculum development will be coherent and follow a clear pattern or pathway. In the previous chapters there has been some emphasis on child development and on the development of others' philosophical stance on education by those such as Bruner and Vygotsky. In the light of your reading and your experiences working with young children, you should try to examine your own ideas and beliefs about what effective education for the young child means. Think about ideas that you have about education, about what you teach, how you teach it and why you teach it.

Developing an understanding of your own position can help you to clarify your goals for teaching and learning and give your work personal meaning and purpose that motivate and energise you. It can help you choose among competing understandings and interpretations of classroom events, provide a basis for discussion about what you are trying to achieve in your workplace with parents and colleagues and develop an agreed team approach (MacNaughton 2003).

Conclusion

In this chapter we have looked at how the curriculum that guides our teaching is dependent not only on our national guidelines but also on your own principles, knowledge and philosophical background, your beliefs about the purposes of education and your understanding of child development. The curriculam should provide a framework for dynamic and holistic practice while your professional understanding of how young children learn and your subject knowledge will provide the exciting learning experiences that children need.

POINTS FOR REFLECTION

Yourself

What is important in teaching:

- the content, or *what* you teach;
- your method, or *how* you teach;
- your ethos, or your *reasons* behind what you teach?

Relate these to the thinking of the educational theorists.

Your practice

A setting reflects the beliefs of practitioners who work there. Evaluate how the space, resources, timetable and organisation reflect their beliefs. (What are their beliefs?)

References

Alexander, R. (1988) *Time for Change: Curriculum Managers at Work*. Warwick and Oxford: Crepe.

Alexander, R. (2000) *Culture and Pedagogy*. Oxford: Blackwell.

Bottle, G. (2003) 'Children's mathematical experiences in the home'. Unpublished Ph.D, University of Kent.

Bruner, J. (1983) *Child's Talk: Learning the Language*. New York: Norton.

David, T. (2001) 'Curriculum in the early years', in G. Pugh (ed.) *Contemporary Issues in the Early Years* (3rd edn). London: Paul Chapman Publishing.

Donaldson, M. (1978) *Children's Minds*. London: Fontana.

Hartley, D. (1993) *Understanding the Nursery School*. London: Cassell.

Lubeck, S. (1985) *Sandbox Society*. Hove: Falmer Press.

Macnaughton, G. (2003) *Shaping Early Childhood*. Berkshire: Open University Press.

Meade, M. (1999) 'If you say it three times then it must be true: critical use of research in early childhood education'. Unpublished paper presented at the 3rd Warwick International Conference of Early Childhood, Warwick University, UK.

Munn, P. and Schaffer, H.R. (1993) 'Literacy and numeracy events in social interactive contexts', *International Journal of Early Years Education*, 1 (3), 61–80.

Nutbrown, C. (1994) *Threads of Thinking: Young Children Learning and the Role of Education*. London: Paul Chapman Publishing.

Pollard, A. (1996) *Readings for Reflective Teaching in Primary Schools*. Milton Keynes: Open University Press.

QCA (2000) *Curriculum Guidance for the Foundation Stage*. London: QCA.

Rogoff, B. (1990) *Apprenticeship in Thinking*. New York: Oxford University Press.

Saxe, G., Guberman, S. and Gearhart, M. (1987) 'Social processes in early number development', quoted in Monograph of the Society for Research in Child Development, 52 (2), serial no 216.

Scrimshaw, P. (1983) *Educational Ideologies*. Milton Keynes: Open University Press.

Tizard, B. and Hughes, M. (1984) *Young Children Learning: Thinking and Talking in the Home*. London: Fontana.

Building confidence

PRINCIPLES . . .

- Children who feel confident about themselves and their ability have a head start in learning.

. . . INTO PRACTICE

- Build an environment where children feel safe to take risks and learn how to resolve conflict.

Self-concept

If children are to be successful learners and well-rounded individuals, then it is important that they develop confidence in a supportive and encouraging atmosphere.

Humans are born explorers; they are curious and have an inbuilt need to know. This natural curiosity can be nurtured or in unfavourable circumstances it can be stifled (Tizard and Hughes 1984).

If children are to develop the confidence that they need to face the challenges of later life, then they must be allowed to take risks and learn how to resolve conflict. This chapter explores the ways in which practitioners can give children the freedom they need to develop confidence in their own abilities while at the same time ensuring that the children are in a safe environment.

Self-concept is the way in which a child perceives him or herself. This perception, or understanding of self-will, determines how a child will behave and react to different circumstances. A child's development is socially and culturally constructed and consequently a child develops their self-concept from the world they inhabit and from the experiences that they have.

Children should be given the opportunity to build up an understanding of themselves, as individuals, so that each one of them can become confident and competent in knowing their own abilities and limitations. If children are to have the confidence to participate in whatever opportunities come their way, then they need to have a positive view of themselves. In order to build up a positive view of oneself, it is necessary to experience success in overcoming the challenges of everyday life and experiences. Success is important as it generates self-assurance, which will in turn lead the child to develop a positive self-concept.

If a child is to grow into a self-assured adult, then one of the important aspects of their progress is the development of confidence in movement. This is part and parcel of growing up, as the child not only learns about their own physical capability but also learns about their own existence in space, their place in the physical world and the relationships between themselves and others. Children will develop confidence in their own physical ability by taking an active part in situations that are challenging to them and give them the chance to succeed or at least partially succeed. Three-year-old James was in the outside area of the nursery. He was trying to walk along a plank. He was very hesitant at first and 'fell off' (always landing on his feet) several times. The practitioner encouraged and challenged James on each attempt by pointing out that he was getting further each time and suggesting that he climb back on and have another go. Because of this encouragement from the practitioner, and James's own determination, each time he fell off he went back to the end of the plank and balanced carefully in order to try again. Each time he attempted the walk he managed to go a little further before falling off. Eventually, when James actually managed to walk to the other end of the plank, he smiled broadly. He was pleased with his physical abilities and would be less hesitant and therefore happier and more confident next time to repeat the experience or to try something new.

James's success in this activity had relied on the physical challenge being available. Practitioners at this setting had decided that the risk of injury from falling from the plank placed about 15 cm above the ground was small, and that the odd stubbed toe or grazed knee was a small price to pay when weighed against the challenge of balancing on the plank. The practitioners decided that a crash mat was not desirable, as it would not allow the children to experience the 'real' risk. The presence of the practitioner ensured that some risks, such as pushing, were nullified. Challenges were set and support was offered for those who were hesitant. Encouragement of the child's independence was important here as too much 'help', such as leading James by the hand, while it would have led to James getting to the end of the plank, would not have given him the feeling of independent success.

Plank walking

Children are not as reckless as we might imagine and will usually be aware of their own abilities and limitations and will enjoy testing out their own physical adeptness. The independence that James was allowed gave him the chance to decide for himself whether he was competent to walk along the plank and to calculate for himself whether engaging in the plank walking activity was worth the risk of falling from it.

Independence

Setting the children challenges and allowing them the opportunity to develop their independence, especially within practical, physically demanding activities, is fraught with dilemmas; not least the consideration of the risks that may be involved. This is because in order for the children to make the most of such opportunities the practitioner will need to allow them to learn independently, by letting them make their own decisions and, more importantly, learn from their own mistakes.

Adults who are less confident about their principles may have a tendency to feel that they must be 'in control' of all aspects of learning. They feel, quite rightly, that they are responsible for what happens in the setting and that

The sheer joy of physical exercise

includes children's safety. It is when children's opportunities to try new things are limited by health and safety considerations that their learning opportunities may become closed down.

When planning activities, practitioners need to be able to make judgements and choices based on calculations of risk, and weigh that risk against the learning opportunities for the children. In order to do this effectively, it is important that we understand ourselves and our reaction to risky experiences. Helen Penn (2005) gives an example of how the concept of risk can be affected by personal fears and experiences and the way in which this can affect our judgement about what is best for the children in our care. She quotes a Berkshire nursery, which as well as offering childcare ran a large training programme for childcare workers, and which had a very small outside walled play yard. The yard was completely empty and the ground was completely covered in black rubber. A freak accident to her own child eleven years earlier had persuaded the nursery manager that the benefits of outdoor play were outweighed by the risk. She felt that it was necessary to provide a completely safe environment and was worried about possible litigation by parents should an accident occur.

Not giving children outside play opportunities is relatively commonplace and I have, on numerous occasions, been to early years settings where practitioners do not let the children go outside on days that they say are 'too cold', 'too wet', 'too snowy', 'too hot' or 'too windy'. This restricts the children's experiences when the provision of suitable protection from the elements, such as warm clothing or a shady area, could allow children to enjoy and learn how to deal with these phenomena first hand. Of course, practitioners should take precautions against sunburn, heatstroke and frostbite, but overprotection can severely limit the children's opportunities to engage in what are for them exciting experiences such as catching snowflakes, stomping in puddles and chasing fallen leaves in the autumn.

Pressure from outside, then, and fears of litigation may have the effect of stifling opportunities. However, if early years education has any principles, the prime one must be to open up learning opportunities for children rather than see them closed down. A balance needs to be struck between keeping children safe and allowing them to experience challenging situations. It is our responsibility to make sure that children are able to participate in all areas of their lives. Allowing children to take some risks, such as using proper tools or climbing and balancing, can help them to make better decisions and can improve their self-awareness. Children who are not given the opportunity to plant bulbs, come into contact with animals or use equipment such as blunt-ended needles, staplers and woodworking implements are not only denied a range of creative experiences but may be less well prepared to deal with potentially hazardous situations when they arise. Research has shown that by preparing children to deal with physical challenges, handle animals sensitively and use tools properly, it helps them to become competent and safe.

Changing society

We are quickly becoming a 'blame and sue' society and in recent years a number of schools have banned traditional playground games in case pupils are hurt while playing games on school premises, which, they fear, might lead to their being sued by angry parents. Games that have been banned include skipping (after some girls fell over), making daisy chains (because of possible germs on the flowers), climbing on climbing frames and football (because it is antisocial). Some schools have banned playing 'conkers' on the grounds that it is dangerous. Teachers are fearful that children may get hit in the eye and that children with nut allergies may be adversely affected. According to the Royal Society for the Prevention of Accidents, however, there is no record of any conker-induced hospital admissions, and the Anaphylaxis Campaign says it is not aware of any severe reactions to conkers among children with nut allergies.

Pupils' viewpoints

The response from young pupils is, of course, difficult to gauge, as they do not really know what they are missing. However, there have been some negative responses by older pupils who are old enough to remember times when such bans were less commonplace. Emma is 13 and from Birmingham.

> The end of playground fun was ages ago at our school! No daisy-chains, no skipping, no running games, no taking paper and pencils outside, last five minutes in the shade on a hot day, no Yo-yos, no football, no staying inside, no sitting down until the last five minutes, no drinking or snacks, no singing or dancing, no shouting or talking, only whispering, no whistling, no laughing; only walking and whispering, not even hand clapping games!

Yasmin, who is 14 and from London, is also upset by the situation.

> In our school we had a really good playground with a long slide, climbing frame, swings, and a large mound type place which you could climb. Now all of that has been taken away for safety reasons. What are people supposed to do at breaktimes?
>
> (CBBC Newsround 2005)

So why are schools worried about children playing games that would not have caused anxiety in the past? Frank Furedi, professor of sociology at the University of Kent, says that conker worries just illustrate that parents are becoming increasingly protective of their children. He calls this phenomenon 'paranoid parenting'. He fears that children are so protected that we risk suffocating them. He is concerned that parents are finding it increasingly difficult to go against the tide of increasing overprotection.

> What I've noticed over the last few years is that occasionally you get a ripple or a backlash and parents are shocked or outraged at how far we're going in overprotecting our children. But then within a short time what was outrageous is seen as 'common sense'. It happened a few years ago when the first schools said they were going to ban parents from videoing nativity plays and football matches at school. At first parents reacted against it, but now they accept it.
>
> (Furedi 2004)

Our fears for children's safety are often out of proportion to the risk and at times our worries are even groundless. We have to accept that freak and tragic accidents will always happen and not allow our fears to overshadow our children's lives to the extent that we stifle creativity, close down their opportunities and even compromise their health. By overprotecting our children from risk of conflict or accident we may be missing the real dangers of obesity and ill health that come as a result of an inactive, risk-free childhood. Practitioners have to balance the need to keep children safe with allowing them to experience, and learn to deal with, danger, fear and even pain. No practitioner likes to see a child hurt but the price of the odd grazed elbow, torn T-shirt, cold feet or cut finger sustained while experiencing a small adventure such as kicking leaves, building in the snow, climbing or using tools can be offset by the big lesson they might learn about how to cope with the risks that are bound to come later.

Other countries and risk

Nurseries in this country vary widely in their approach to the risks that their children are allowed to take. But typically children are not allowed to play fight in case they hurt each other, climb for fear they might fall, use tools in case they stab or cut themselves or go outside when it is cold.

This cautious approach was highlighted for me the other day when some postgraduate students were asked to plan an outside play area for a preschool setting. One group decided to plan an area on the theme of a builder's yard. It was suggested that a few real bricks and thermalite blocks could be provided for the children to handle and use to build low walls. Another student immediately said that this was unacceptable as any wall they built might fall on the children. Some strong argument followed to justify why children should not be allowed real building materials of any sort. The argument was based on the safety of the children and comments such as 'the children might play fight with the plastic plumbing pipes and hurt each other', 'they might get splinters from the wood' and 'they might throw the sand which might go in their eyes' were made. The idea of a workbench with tools was completely dismissed by a number of the students. The students found it so easy to get carried away with the health and safety of the pupils that they completely lost sight of any benefits that such an experience might bring. There was one student, though, brave enough to challenge this thinking. She said that as long as there were not enough bricks for the children to build a wall high enough for it to fall and crush them underneath and as long as ground rules were explained to the children so that they knew what was expected of them, then the odd splinter or bruised toe would be acceptable. Some felt that parents would not find any injury to their child acceptable. This argument remained largely unresolved, with each side convinced that their own position was the right one. Observations of different settings will provide a full range of approaches. This makes formulating a safety policy of one's own a difficult business. It is fair to say that the practioner needs their own experience in a setting to build the confidence to form that policy.

Play fighting has long been discouraged in preschools in this country. This still seems to be the case even though it is now known that this type of roughhouse play is a natural part of growing up and that it can have a positive effect on children as it allows them to rehearse the ways that they can deal with conflict in a safe and relatively harmless way. Contrary to popular belief, it seems that children are able to distinguish between play and reality. They can be seen to step out of role in order to look after another child who may have been hurt, report a problem to a practitioner or comfort a friend for whom the rough and tumble has become too much. Practitioners in other cultures do not necessarily react to play fighting in the same way and see it simply as a part of growing up. Mary Jane Drummond (1993) cites the case of a Japanese boy, which demonstrates a difference in cultural expectation surrounding play fighting. When Horoki, a four-year-old boy, came close to other children, he punched, poked and wrestled with them, even leaving his post as monitor at the organ during the pre-lunch song to wrestle with a child nearby. After his dinner he enjoyed rough-house play with a small group of boys. The response from the Japanese practitioners to Horoki's behaviour was 'If there were no fights among our four-year-old children that would be a real problem. We don't encourage children to fight, but children need to fight when they are young if they are to develop into complete human beings.'

Children in preschool settings in England are often not allowed to go outside when it is cold for fear of it being detrimental to their health and are rarely taken off the premises to ensure their safety. In other countries, particularly Scandinavia, children are positively encouraged to enjoy the outside and even risky pastimes. In Finland children are required to spend part of their day outside, and on a visit to Helsinki I witnessed groups of preschoolers, positioned along a rope, on their daily trek to the local play park with their early years practitioners. Here the children could be seen playing on climbing frames, seesaws, swings and rope swings and walking along raised logs. Slightly older children could be seen, seemingly unsupervised, in the early morning before school, climbing on wooden climbing frames provided in their school playground. The children were sure-footed and the joy of the physical exercise was obvious. Finnish children are also introduced to cross-country skiing and tobogganing in the winter. Similarly, children in Norway have outside camps, whatever the weather, and the emphasis is on the children learning to adapt to the environment rather than adjusting the environment for the safety of the children. In this country, in contrast, children are typically not allowed to go out in the snow during school time in case they get cold and wet.

Safety at the expense of health

There are two main areas where health might be compromised if the possibility of risk is thought by practitioners to outweigh the benefits. The first is the lack of exercise and the second is to do with excessive cleaning.

Studies carried out in Canada and Australia (Penn 2005) indicate that children in these countries are usually encouraged not to take risks, as are children in this country. This overcautiousness has led to immobility and lack of exercise, which seems to be leading to an increased number of children suffering from childhood obesity. It seems possible that this might also be the case here, as childhood obesity and its attendant health problems, such as diabetes, are on the increase.

Everyone would agree that a safe and hygienic environment is important, but just as children's minds need to adapt in their thinking and learning by encountering novel situations, their bodies also need to learn to adapt to new situations too. Oversensitivity to issues of hygiene, resulting in overzealous cleaning, can mean that children do not meet the small exposures to bacteria and viruses that help to develop their immune systems. From a medical standpoint, the development of an efficient physiological system for each of us depends, at least in part, on small exposures to bacteria and viruses so that young bodies can adapt to changing environments.

Health and safety training

Early years practitioners in any setting have a duty to keep their children safe from harm and to ensure that health and safety issues are dealt with. Risk assessment is a routine part of planning and practitioners have a duty to be up to date with the school's emergency policies.

All adults working in settings are required to have health and safety training. Practitioners are competent professionals who know their children well. This knowledge of children's capabilities and preferences will help practioners to develop a balanced view of the risks that the children face, particularly from accidental injury and death. The competent experienced practitioner will be well placed to balance exploration with risk and to make decisions which will protect children from harm while at the same time giving them strategies to extend their range of abilities. Demonstrating confidence in young children, while teaching them safe practices, is a most effective way forward in ensuring that children develop the independence they need.

Putting risk into perspective

In order to make informed decisions, it is important that risk is put into perspective and what follows might help the practitioner to bring an informed view to any decisions made. The sobering news is that accidental injury is the biggest single cause of death in UK in children over the age of one and that in 2002, 320 children aged under 15 died as the result of injury or poisoning. It is also true to say that more children die each year as the result of accidents than from illnesses such as leukaemia or meningitis. Every year over 2 million children are taken to a hospital after having an accident. On a more positive note, the number of children's accidents has been declining steadily from 2.5 million in 1997 to 2.1 million in 2002 and accidental death has also shown a steady fall. These figures refer to all accidents, including those at home, so do not give a true picture of what is happening within settings. There is little information that relates purely to preschool settings but it is true to say from figures that are available that accidents in preschool settings are fewer than in mainstream school.

Accident prevention

Preschool groups are expected to provide a health and safety policy and, as already said, it is incumbent on practitioners to ensure the safety of the children in their settings. There is also legislation which relates to child safety. These regulations ensure that the products we buy meet a reasonable level of safety performance and that new dwellings meet an acceptable level of safety.

There are a number of organisations that can help practitioners and parents understand better the risks and consequences of accidents. Two of these organisations are the Child Accident Prevention Trust and RoSPA (Royal Society for the Prevention of Accidents).

Child Accident Prevention Trust

The Child Accident Prevention Trust (www.capt.org.uk) is a national charity committed to reducing the number of children and young people killed, disabled or seriously injured as a result of accidents. The main thrust of its activity is to provide information for parents and practitioners that will help them in the prevention of accidents.

The Royal Society for the Prevention of Accidents (RoSPA)

RoSPA (www.rospa.org.uk) believe that 'A safe, secure and sustainable environment is a prerequisite for a healthy nation.' They believe that there are four aspects to accident prevention that have to be considered. These are:

- environment
- education
- empowerment
- enforcement.

Health promotion

In line with *Every Child Matters,* children centres and SureStart settings are expected not only to have a health and safety policy but also to comply with the new *National Service Framework (NSF) for Children, Young People and Maternity*

Services (DfES and Department of Health 2004) and to take a more holistic view of health and safety which includes health promotion.

Child Accident Prevention is seen to be 'underpinned by a health promotion programme, based on best available evidence, that focuses on priority issues such as healthy eating, physical activity, safety, smoking, sexual health and mental health, and is delivered by all practitioners who come into contact with children and young people, and in all settings used by this age group' (DfES and DH 2004: 29).

Children gaining confidence

Children gain confidence when they are challenged at a level where they can expect to be successful. Usually this success is achieved through a combination of the help from an 'expert other' and practice. Children will often want to share their successes by shouting 'Look at me' when they have reached the top of the climbing frame or the end of a balancing beam. They rightfully feel a sense of achievement when they have understood a new story or worked out how many pieces of apple are needed for each member of the group.

Confidence in other areas of development is sometimes less straightforward to identify and to achieve. As Jennie Lindon (2005) says, 'The same head that is coming to grips with the meaning of number or that some squiggles are "writing", is also trying to make sense of social situations and the behaviour of others.' Aptitude at balancing or counting is no guarantee of success in the complex inter-change of social relationships that must be negotiated each day in the setting but there is a common factor that helps children have confidence in their own ability to succeed in all their endeavours. The child who has a strong sense of their iden-tity and a sense of well-being is the child who will approach relationships with sensitivity and have the belief that they have some influence, or agency, over things that happen to them.

We consider relationships in some depth in Chapter 9 but it is worth consider-ing here that it is this sense of identity that shapes a child's concept of their ability to engage in deep relationships with other children. How children see themselves in terms of 'worthwhile' or 'worthless' has its roots in early infancy and is part of the perception of self which grows from the mirroring process of reciprocal relationships within the family. Children bring this image of them-selves to the setting and project it into their relationships with others. Their feel-ings about themselves also influence the ways in which they respond to their environment, leading either to a confident approach to representing their feel-ings and ideas or to a helpless approach which requires constant approval from others and a tendency to give up easily. A child with a strong sense of identity knows that they are special and understands their own feelings, how to deal with them and how to express them appropriately. This child can deal confidently with the conflicts which can easily arise in the busy setting because they know that reasoned debate is a powerful tool and one that is acceptable in this environment. Moreover, it is the tool that they have probably had experience of using at home. The child with a poor sense of identity is more likely to be less verbally confident, finding communication difficult because of the previous experiences of not being listened to. This child may be conformist and compliant but may also be attention seeking and use confrontation as a way of being noticed. The wise educator will allocate as long as it takes to giving the unconfident child the words and phrases that are useful in the setting to get what they need, remembering that so-called 'unreasonable behaviour' is always reasonable from the point of view of the child displaying it. Phrases such as 'please may I have that when you have finished' can be used to great effect by very young children, and once the culture of asking and requesting is well established, children themselves will help to spread the 'articulacy culture' which is a skill that will be useful all their lives.

Modelling respectful behaviour will also increase an unconfident child's self-image. As successful experiences in negotiation increase within a supportive environment, the unconfident child will be able to express themselves better not only in gathering resources they need but in expressing their thoughts and feelings appropriately.

The child whose sense of identity is strengthened in this way will begin to develop a better sense of purpose and will try new ventures with enthusiasm. This is the point that Jennie Lindon (2005) describes as 'where feeling meets thinking' as she considers the positive dispositions that children need to possess to encourage them to persevere, to succeed and to risk failure.

Confidence is more likely to be developed in a setting where the learning is playful and children can make decisions that may not lead to success. In play, this is an acceptable part of learning something new; there are no right and wrong answers and so confidence is built up as children practise and review what they do until they are satisfied with the results. An environment which is overdependent on outcome measures that are set by adults necessarily has right and wrong answers which only the adults know about. Children who constantly experience answering closed questions that seem meaningless and have nothing to do with their own intentions are likely to begin to feel more 'worthless' than 'worthwhile' as the wrong answers accumulate. As disaffection grows, children may no longer feel that school learning is for them and the resultant lack of confidence and poor self-image can affect people all their lives.

The early years setting, then, has a wonderful opportunity, and indeed a duty, to build confidence in very young children who are often thought of as incompetent. We know that, given the supportive, challenging environment they deserve, they have enormous potential to form loving friendships, negotiate what they need and debate the fairness of moral dilemmas. They have the right to expect that we will support them to become confident and articulate people.

Conclusion

We have thought about the part that children's self-esteem plays in their ability to participate fully in the opportunities we offer them or that they may encounter in the future. Confidence in the building of effective relationships stands children in good stead for the rest of their lives.

POINTS FOR REFLECTION

Yourself

Look at your own ideas about the tension that exists between challenging activities and keeping children safe. Evaluate your own views about ensuring a realistic balance.

Your practice

Define and introduce strategies you and your team could use to help children in developing assertive yet caring relationships with all those that they encounter.

References

CBBC Newsround (2005) http://news.bbc.co.uk/cbbcnews/hi/chat/your_comments/newsid_2158000/2158826.stm (accessed October 2005).

DfES and DH (2004) *National Service Framework for Children, Young People and Maternity Services.* London: HMSO.

Drummond, M.J. (1993) *Assessing Children's Learning.* London: David Fulton Publishers.

Furedi, F. (2004) 'Paranoid parenting', *Guardian*, 20 October.

Penn, H. (2005) *Understanding Early Childhood Issues and Controversies.* Buckingham: Open University Press.

Lindon, J. (2005) *Understanding Child Development.* London: Hodder Arnold.

Tizard, B. and Hughes, M. (1984) *Young Children Learning: Talking and Thinking at Home.* London: Fontana.

Learning about self and others

- Play and conversation are the main ways in which children learn about themselves and others.

- Recognise that the high quality of adults' interaction with children helps to move learning forward. It is by watching what they do and listening to what they say that children tell us what they know.

Play and conversation

The Rumbold Report (DES 1990) set out three approaches to learning that are central to the notion of 'Starting with Quality' in early year settings. These three approaches are to do with: play, talk and the role of the adult. Rumbold emphasises that facilitating play and talk requires high quality adult interactions with children. To help us think about how this level of interaction takes place, we need to unpick the meaning of 'quality' in terms of the adult's role. The report implies quality is composed of such factors as practitioners building trusting and secure relationships. Such relationships, where the child feels valued and respected, will enable them to take risks, make mistakes, tackle new problems and overcome minor difficulties within the personal safety net of warm, attentive, caring adults. Part of the process of developing respectful relationships will include practitioners being actively aware of their influence as role models and so taking opportunities to pattern positive attitudes to diversity. If experiences are planned, having observed children's interests and needs and with high expectations of their abilities, it will add to the quality of relationship the practitioner builds with children, their parents and other important people involved in their development.

Aspects of conversation

The *Effective Provision of Preschool Education* (Sylva *et al.* 2004) is the first major longitudinal study of a national sample of young children's intellectual and social development between the ages of 3 and 7 years. Key findings from the project are largely compatible the qualitative factors on adult–child interactions identified in *Starting with Quality* (DES 1990): 'The quality of interactions between children and staff were particularly important; where staff showed warmth and were responsive to the individual needs of children, children made more progress' (Sylva *et al.* 2003).

If we work from the premise that human relationship relies on a reciprocal process of communication, we begin to see how verbal and non-verbal communication in the form of play and talk can contribute to children's personal, social and emotional development. Significantly, it is when play and talk are seen as symbolic forms that their potential for extending children's imaginative, creative potential in all areas of learning becomes most apparent.

Play, talk and observation

Play is a slippery concept. There are many types and many levels of play that have been written about extensively by early years educators such as Isaacs, Bruce, Nutbrown and Moyles. Child-initiated play is similar to, or at least compatible with, developing language competence. The practitioner's role in providing quality experiences for young children is similar. The first assumption is that child-initiated play and talk are both symbolic functions. Play assumes children are able to manipulate objects in the environment that may represent something else, for example cardboard boxes for houses, cars, shops. Talk assumes children are able to manipulate words that represent objects, people or experiences. The second assumption is that play is intrinsically motivated, freely chosen, non-literal and actively and voluntarily engaged in for pleasure, and in the early years setting this is usually also the case with talk.

In our culture, playing with words informs a long literary heritage that chronicles the spiritual heights and emotional depths of the human condition; it is this that language can help us explore. This form of catharsis can work from the ritualised utterances of early nursery and playground rhymes, through narrative, to the high drama and poetry of Shakespeare. Words, beyond their outline shape, trigger thoughts, feelings and ideas that can contribute to the way we experience ourselves and how we experience others. Such is the social, symbolic power of language that speaking and listening, reading and writing remain a core aim of teaching and learning. The primary function is to initiate children into common language and literacy practices that essentially embody current cultural practices. Ironically, in our culture, this compatibility between play and talk in terms of creative potential has been largely overlooked, as literacy and language are highly revered, while play is largely seen as an unimportant preoccupation of early years enthusiasts. However, there are signs that government is beginning to perceive that a relationship between social and emotional learning and the creative thinking processes is required to ensure all children achieve their potential (DfES 1999, 2002, 2003a, 2003b).

The task of the practitioner in the early years setting is to tune into and build upon the child's existing experience. Those experiences will manifest themselves in behaviours that can be observed in the early years setting as talk and play. The practitioner needs to be confident about the value of observing children as the key to understanding and developing these experiences.

Enhancing quality experience in terms of interactions or relationships between the child and the adult is to do with ensuring that the 'continuity, reciprocity, identity' children have enjoyed in their earliest experiences is developed in the early years setting. To do this effectively, practitioners need to have the confidence to position themselves as learners in order to find out about the children in their care. If we are trying to find out about where a child is socially, emotionally, intellectually and physically, and if we are looking for places where we can begin to develop 'shared and sustained thinking', a tick in a box on an observation sheet will not suffice. To ensure sound beginnings there is no substitute for authentic engagement. Authentic engagement is about talking and playing, but it is also about reflecting on and evaluating those actions. Observation, by watching children's play and listening to children's conversations, is central to that reflective,

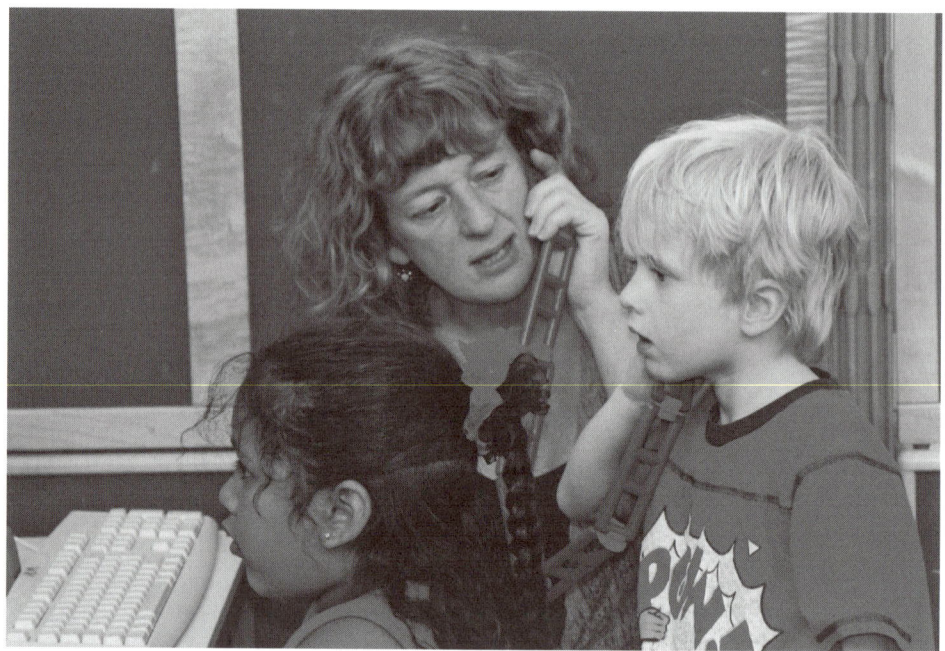

Quality interaction between children and the staff

problem-solving, assessment process: 'Observation is taking time to hear and see what a child seems to be doing, feeling, thinking. A practitioner observes, then documents' (Dahlberg *et al.* 1999, quoted in Pugh 2001). This 'documentation' provides material for reflective discussion and dialogue with colleagues, parents and other professionals about children's positive dispositions, strengths, difficulties, interactions with others and self-esteem. Collaborative practitioner discourse provides the basis for planning and making decisions about actions to support and extend children's learning. Observation is central to this pedagogical level of attentive thought, talk and action. This supports continuity for children by reflecting some of the containing qualities children experience in family life. It also models for children the 'shared, sustained thinking' implicit in quality relationships.

Play and creativity

Winnicott (1971) talks of play being a primary source of creativity. For Winnicott a baby at birth is unable to differentiate between the object that is himself and the object that is his mother. The process of building a separate identity can be supported by what he terms a 'transitional' object or phenomenon in the form first of a thumb, then a favoured blanket, teddy or toy. This object, which must almost always be close to hand, becomes a vital part of the child's daily routines and rituals, and represents an intermediate stage of coming to terms with its inner world and outer reality. Significantly the infant 'assumes rights' and ownership over the object and can use it to explore a range of emotions and feelings from loving hugs to kicking and pulling apart, which the loved and hated object usually manages to survive. In this way, 'reality-testing' can be undertaken in a safe, secure space that is neither inside the child nor outside in the world at large, but involves active experience with a chosen object. As the child develops a more mature sense of self, the need for the transitional object gradually disappears, but the important link here is between transitional phenomena, play and wider experience: 'There is a direct development from transitional phenomena to playing, and from playing to shared playing, and from this to cultural experiences.' (Winnicott 1971: 151).

Transitional phenomena in relation to play can be interpreted as 'spaces' where children can engage in activities by investing their imagination and manipulating objects in a safe environment. Engaging playfully in this way depends on the child's confidence in their own ability to manipulate their environment. It also depends on the level of trust the child has in the adults who create those transitional spaces for play. This trust will arise from the observational interest, attentive listening, engagement through presence and time given to talk that the adults have consistently offered. This kind of emotional holding experience offered by practitioners in the early years settings echoes those earliest childhood experiences of 'good enough' adaptive mothering. In the early years setting, when a reciprocal sense of trust is secured, which of course is dependent on the quality of relationship nurtured in the preschool, nursery or Reception class, the practitioner has the privileged opportunity of entering the child's imaginative world.

> The potential space between baby and mother, between child and family, between individual and society or the world depends on experience that leads to trust. It can be looked upon as sacred to the individual in that it is here that the individual experiences creative living.
>
> (Winnicott 1967, quoted in Holmes 2001)

The observant, attentive practitioner is able to tap into the child's (sub)consciousness, the child's world, and their real and imagined experiences by observing the social mediation of talk through play. This will help the practitioner to think and talk about ways of developing the child's interests and experiences and extending positive dispositions for learning. It will also help the practitioner think about creating transitional space in the setting, in the child and in the practioner's mind.

Finding potentially creative spaces for play and talk

The notion of 'space' is an important theme that recurs in our experience, as well as in current research when thinking about play and talk. Should we intervene in children's talk and play? When should intervention take place? There is necessarily a time implication when thinking about 'space' for creative play and talk in this way. What are the optimum levels of control and contingency? These are the pedagogical questions the practitioner is constantly engaged in. The level of intervention the practitioner engages in will impact on the child's creative play and talk, and therefore quality of learning experience. Students researching adult support in activities with young children are repeatedly surprised to report that when compared to non-intervention, the child's talk is inhibited by the intervention, direction or control of the teacher, who has specific outcomes for the activity in mind.

Ben is nearly five and struggles to understand and to articulate words. He has a warm, concerned family and is an active, affectionate little boy with a sense of fun. He has competently communicated his personality to other children and staff. The Reception class is a demanding space for Ben because it is so often ordered and regulated by the language of instruction. In organised situations arranged to support Ben's language development he quickly becomes tired, restless and is easily distracted. The discomfort and frustrations he feels when unable to perform are palpable. However, Ben likes to make things and to paint, and when freed from the formal demands of learning to be literate, he gravitates to the painting area in the classroom and 'plays'. It is at these times, when totally absorbed in his painting, that Ben talks. He is relaxed and comfortably engaged in a physical, sensory action over which he feels he has some control. In charge of his own thoughts and actions, tension is diminished and as he becomes rapt in the flow and freedom of his actions, he engages in 'self-talk'. The literal space he has found in this environment and the free-flow play in which he engages open a space in Ben's mind where he is secure and feels safe enough, as in Winnicott's 'transitional space', to risk or to dare to practise out loud all those sounds and words he struggles with when someone else puts him on the spot and tries to transmit knowledge about language.

The practitioner's role here is to listen to and to observe Ben, to record all the valuable knowledge, experience and understanding that he actually has in order to utilise it to extend his learning. This could be done by talking about the shape of his irregular language (sounds, words, structures, meanings) with colleagues who work with him, and other professionals such as the speech and language therapist. They need to talk about the content of Ben's 'self-talk' with the real experts, his parents, to identify 'home-language' that has significant meanings for Ben. This will initiate a valuable dialogue and link and create continuity between the cultures of home and school. Ben will begin to discern a relationship between himself, his family and teachers that will help him make sense of himself in his new surroundings.

Practitioners should use the insights that listening, observation and home communication bring to incorporate some of Ben's talk into their everyday interactions with him, thus truly meeting the child on his own ground and providing an authentic platform for new learning. This will undoubtedly help him feel valued, specifically included and held in mind by these new people who are not his family. He will also be respected for what he is able to bring to the new group. His popularity indicates his peers have already competently tapped into Ben's way of communicating. The practitioner could take the opportunity of matching Ben's dispositions with those of other children to work in a small group. His peers could model apt talk for Ben, but they may also learn from his warmth and humour, thus extending mutually beneficial learning. The practitioners' listening and observation needs to be a continual revelation informing 'sustained and shared thinking' with each other, with Ben and with his parents. This reflective talk or discourse should surround plans for accommodating Ben's creative dispositions through talk and multisensory play in a more organic, holistic way than discrete teaching permits.

The theme of creating appropriate spaces to facilitate processes of talking, thinking and playing during the creative process is particularly important in the Reggio Emilia approach. Nurse (2001) talks of nurseries being light, spacious, beautiful structures that combine small intimate places for talk and large light-filled spaces where children work collaboratively on projects developed from their interests, ideas and enthusiasm, using a wide range of natural, found and art materials. These spaces echo an approach that is about giving time and space to talk and to reflect on shared, creative play. In our curriculum-driven educational culture, children's experiences are often activity led rather than personalised or learner centred, even in some early years settings. In such settings time and space is measured by the practitioner's extrinsic timetabled agenda. Time on task is the aim. This can leave little space literally, emotionally or cognitively for the child to take control, to initiate play and talk in a creative, autonomous way.

Off-task activity is often viewed negatively and associated with inappropriate behaviours or even idleness. However, if we reflect on our own learning, it soon becomes clear that our best understanding does not actually occur during a frenzy of 'doing'. It is often when the action has ceased, during 'down-time', like Ben in his painting 'space'. This is the time and space to reflect on experience that creatively encourages new learning to emerge. Claxton (1997) talks of the way creativity is enhanced by states of reverie and imagery, and Loveless (2005) suggests 'Such states are not just "letting it flow" . . . but acknowledging a way of knowing which is not necessarily conscious and draws upon resources of knowledge, skill and experience in order to make new combinations, explorations and transformations.'

Language as the currency of meaning-making and cultural mediation

The work of language and literacy researchers such as Cox (1998), Wells (1986) and Meek (1988) enforces the value of using language to make meanings. To reinforce the importance of this in relation to early years settings, it might be

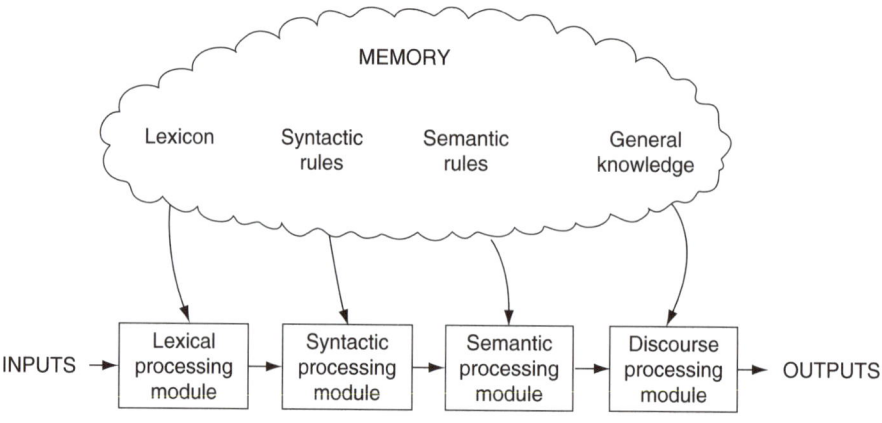

Figure 5.1 A linear model of language processing

Source: Greene and Coulson 1995

helpful to look at some of the complex ways language works. A rudimentary understanding of this from a cognitive perspective will show the importance of meaning-making and its relationship to surviving in a social world. It will also reveal its role in empowering play. Firstly, differentiating four parts and functions of language will help us identify different 'talk' values. Greene and Coulson (1995) give useful definitions:

- **lexis** – all languages have words, a vocabulary or lexicon
- **syntax** – this is about the grammatical structure of language and word order
- **semantic** – this is about meaning-making and contains pragmatics of language
- **discourse** – social talk that is dynamic, interactive and context specific where we contribute our general understanding and knowledge.

Coulson's definitions, looked at in this way (see Figure 5.1), describe a linear process starting from the smallest units of meaning (sounds, words) to the more complex discoursal levels of understanding. This is reminiscent of the current structured approach to literacy for five-year-olds in schools (*National Literacy Strategy*, DfES 2000). In terms of approaches to reading:

- **Lexis** represents a phonics teaching, or phonological awareness training, level of engagement. In terms of meaning-making this is not always helpful as isolated sounds and symbols only carry meaning when embedded or contextualised more broadly within a story, or at least in a sentence relating to the child's experience.
- **Syntax** denotes engagement at grammatical, sentence level. Examples of this would be the three-year-old who says 'Did you wented shopping, Daddy?' and the six-year-old who writes 'Daddy wented shopping'.

Noam Chomsky (1957) was interested in the structure of language and argued that the fragmented nature of conversations babies and young children are exposed to would not be sufficient for the child to deduce a complex adult system. He asserts that language is innate and universal and that our internal Language Acquisition Device determines human language competence as natural. More recent research by linguists suggests that beyond the rudiments of vocabulary (lexis) and grammar (syntax), social interaction is essential to support and develop higher order meaning-making. In terms of building rela-tionships which, as discussed earlier, are essentially social activities and vital to quality interactions between children and staff, the meaning-making semantic and discoursal functions of language are then key.

- **Semantics** deals with higher order language skills, that are about understand-ing and making meaning from what is being said or read.
- **Discourse** is about the talker or reader mediating and interpreting meaning through the social or cultural experience they bring to the conversation, to experience or to text. This represents the text level work in terms of the Literacy Hour.

Central to semantic meaning-making are pragmatics. This is about learning the rules of conversation. These rules involve understanding and drawing meanings from social interactions. It involves aspects of conversation such as turn-taking, being able to maintain and sustain interactions, being able to accommodate the listener to ensure effective communication, and utilising social politeness formu-lae. In this way, pragmatics also concerns the cultural understandings we have taken in through experience that, in turn, helps us to understand the anomalies and ambiguities of our complex language. These understandings may be specific to the culture in which we live. Generally speaking children explore the anom-alies and endless ambiguities of our complex language through trial and error in their daily interactions with siblings, parents, peers and teachers, where errors become part of adaptive play and creative cultural ritual. Many of us retain and cherish child-versions for names of actions, events or things as communal touch-stones of warm, intimate family life. These linguistic points of reference help us make sense of who we are in relation to those who know and care about us (Winnicott 1971; Bruner 1986; Vygotsky 1962) These connections can help us to learn about and value ourselves and help us to develop positive dispositions towards others.

Being able to accommodate a listener, sustain interactions and understand the rules of conversations are so embedded in meaning-making, effective com-munication and engagement for learning that, as practitioners, we cannot afford to overlook their importance. It is when we consider children on the autistic continuum that the importance of this high order functioning of language becomes most apparent. Brian is a five-year-old child with Asperger's syndrome. Being able to read the words on every page of his favourite picture book is a source of great joy for him and his family, but beyond literally describing the colour, shape or form of pictures on the pages, Brian is unable to understand, make sense of or infer even the simplest meaning from the words he reads.

Jamie, who has high order pragmatic-semantic difficulties, has learned how to greet visitors. His script (Schank and Abelson 1977, quoted in Eysenck and Keane 2000) is initially impressive as he takes the initiative by saying 'Hello and welcome! My name is Jamie and how are you?' The guest is impressed, answers Jamie's question, and follows through with additional conversational information and questions. The guest is perplexed, however, as there is no further response from Jamie who is attached to the computer screen instead, unable to accommodate or sustain a dynamic, two-way conversation in this way. Jamie's difficulties manifest themselves linguistically as he is unable to digest and process information and express himself. This may be a long-term memory problem or an inability to draw on schemas, or a combination of both.

A central function of schemas, or mental representations of physical actions, is that they allow us to form expectations using our memory. This happens by matching old learning with new similar experiences, which describes concept formation and intellectual growth. Piaget would see this as part of the 'assimilation-accommodation' process, that is, a cognitive struggle that the individual resolves, more or less, on their own. Vygotsky would see this cognitive dissonance between assimilation and accommodation as representing the 'zone of proximal development', giving an ideal opportunity for adult intervention. Bruner would also conceptualise this gap as an opportunity for bridging or 'scaffolding' by the interactive engagement of an adult tuned into the child's conceptual development stage. The adult, together with the child, would co-construct and develop new meanings from the shared experience. The way we process new experiences is to draw on existing internal mental representations to infer new meanings.

Without the long-term memory organising and storing categories of experience we would experience every action, event or stimulus as though it were for the first time, without connecting or making meanings. The key point for the practitioner is that language is a central cognitive function, bound to memory and concept formation, and therefore essential to development and learning. In early years settings, the conversations we have with children should always work to help them make connections with previous experiences and events. Reminding them of what they know already will accommodate creative spaces for meaning-making and extend their learning experiences.

As mentioned above, language and meanings are fluid, ambiguous and provisional, so meaning is almost always dependent on social and cultural contexts. For example, the expression 'I need some bread' could be taken from a 'Children in Need' advertisement, could refer to a drug-dealing gangster demanding money at gunpoint, or could refer to someone helping to construct the weekly shopping list. Clark (1992) suggested that listeners can only understand talk if they have prior knowledge of the topic under discussion which confirms the role of context, or previous experience, to understanding. Practitioners need to keep constantly in mind that if meanings are negotiated through the contextually defined medium of language, the context of the setting may be different from the child's home culture, ethnicity, gender, social experience and expectations.

Young children are constantly engaged in making bridging inferences (Clark 1992) to help them make sense of the environments and social contexts in which they find themselves. Take the example: 'It's raining . . . fruit in the circle today.' What knowledge of an early years setting is required to make sense of this statement? Without direct reference to the topic of wet playtime procedures in a Reception classroom, children would be left to 'bridge', or fill in the meaning gaps. The social implications for a child with pragmatic-semantic difficulties, and the way that impacts on their emotional well-being, are enormous. But with all children, sensitive awareness of the social, emotional and intellectual implications of language will empower the child to take risks with their thoughts, feelings and words, towards a more shared understanding of cross-cultural meanings.

If development actually worked in a linear cumulative way, observing and planning for children's progress would be a much less complicated task for practitioners. However, an interactive model of language processing acknowledges some of the social and cultural complexities involved by emphasising the way higher order processing (at semantic and discoursal levels) is in a state of perpetual interaction with low order (word and grammar) levels of processing. In this model, processing is multi-directional and each type of language knowledge can influence and draw on other types. Greene and Coulson's diagrams (Figures 5.1 and 5.2) clearly illustrate the difference between a linear and an interactive model of language understanding.

Language, not simply as a tool of communication but as a culturally value-laden vehicle for meaning-making, is essentially social and provides the dialectic base for early years pedagogy. The EPPE report (Sylva *et al.* 2003) confirms, in terms of quality adult–child interactions:

> More 'sustained shared thinking' was observed in settings where children made the most progress. 'Sustained shared thinking' occurs when two or more individuals 'work together' in an intellectual way to solve a problem, clarify a concept, evaluate an activity, extend a narrative etc. Both parties must contribute to the thinking and it must develop and extend understanding.

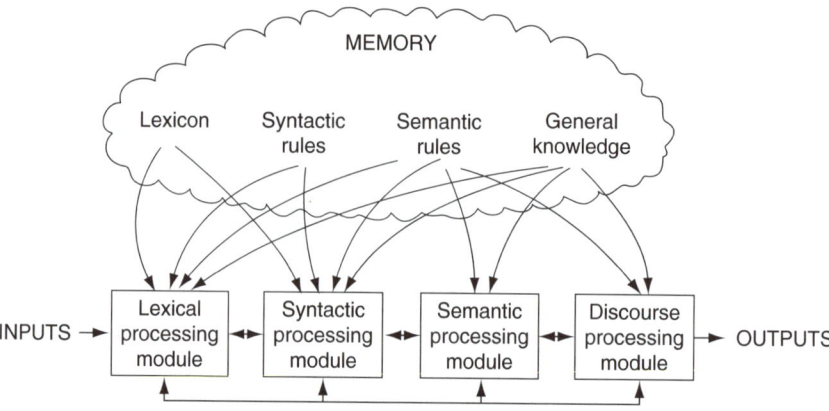

Figure 5.2 An interactive model of language processing

Source: Greene and Coulson 1995

Language and thought, then, are closely related. Vygotsky saw language as a social activity that supports thought through problem solving. Bruner interprets what happens between the supporting adult and the learner in Vygotsky's idea of the 'zone of proximal development'. He asks how the adult lends their understanding to the child and suggests there is a kind of 'scaffold' of consciousness erected by the adult that is borrowed by the learner and accessed through language. This can be exemplified in the rituals, routines, habits and games that are built up in the family context during mealtimes, bath times and bedtime book-sharing. By starting from the child and engaging in play talk that co-constructs meaning at just the right level, the mother plays her part by remaining 'on the growing edge of the child's competence' (Sylva *et al.* 2003).

This reciprocal linguistic and emotional communication helps to give the child a secure sense of self and the confidence to try out these meanings in new contexts with other people to explore further what language can do. This may well take place through play. When sharing a picture book with her younger sister Elizabeth who is three years old, Ellie rehearses the words, timings and tone she recalls from when she read the book at about the same age. She prompts at what she understands are opportune moments, supporting her sister in a similar way to the way her mother supported her when they shared the same story. Vygotsky (1962) might have said that Ellie's mother provided an opportunity for her to 'achieve her own consciousness' beyond the initial support she offered. This process can be extended and utilised in the early years setting by practitioners who realise the learning potential of talk and play.

Bruner (1986) extended Vygotsky's ideas about the social construction of language by proposing that language and thought are regulated by specific cultural practices, as the above examples suggest. He responded to the nativist notion of

Chomsky's Language Acquisition Device by asserting the presence of a Language Acquisition Support System, provided by the child's socio-cultural context, that 'helps the child navigate across the zone of proximal development to full and conscious control of language'. In this way both Bruner and Vygotsky saw the role of adults as essential in relation to talk and play and the child's understanding of him or herself in relation to others.

When children are given appropriate spaces to play and talk collaboratively, they can contribute all their experience, understanding and associations to creatively construct talk that incorporates a rich intertext of meaning. The following example of this is the result of practitioners using children's interest in the story of the three little pigs to initiate a collaborative project. This involved the children in creating an interactive display to facilitate their conversation and play.

DARREN: Let's go to the apple field at 10 o'clock to beat the wolf.

PAUL: No, let's go at 6 cos it'll be dark.

TIM: Then we won't be able to see him, that's dangerous.

PAUL: Yes, we will, there's a moon.

GREG: (*as the wolf arrives at the apple field*) I'll huff and I'll puff and I'll blow your house down!

TIM: No, no don't do that, I'll let you in the window. *Slight pause.*

GREG: No, silly, you're not supposed to do that, I'm meant to get stuck in the chimney!

DARREN: You're not fat enough, we need a different wolf.

TIM: Help, help, the wolf's after me!

DARREN: Where?

TIM: He's coming down the chimney, but getting stuck, like Father Christmas.

PAUL: I'll pull him down.

GREG: No, then I'll eat you up, silly.

TIM: I'm scared.

GREG: It's all right, I only eat pigs sometimes. I'm eating apples today . . .

There is much for the practitioner to observe and to learn here. Darren initiates the excitement and tension intrinsic to imaginative play. He feels safe and secure enough to embark on an unknown journey with his friends. Paul daringly adds the mysterious ingredient of 'darkness' to increase the risk involved in the 'reality check' transitional play spaces allow. Tim is quickly imaginatively and emotionally immersed in the play, but expresses his fears about the dark and the danger and the threatening chant of the wolf. The 'pause' indicates his intensity as the others try to work out why Tim would let the wicked wolf in through the window. His level of engagement also perhaps triggers other fears about Father Christmas getting stuck in the chimney. The introduction of Santa into the play text at this point is problematic. Paul's positive associations with Father Christmas prompt his action to rescue, but Greg, still in touch with the storyline, is able to make bridging inferences and reminds the others of the consequences of the wolf entering the home. Perhaps Greg's abilities to infer meaning are also linked to his ability to empathise. Greg senses he has renewed Tim's fear of the wolf and maturely reassures him that he 'only eats apples today'. From this complex intertext of play and talk emerges an imaginative leap that turns the life-threatening wolf into a benign apple-eating Santa. In this creative, emotional interaction the children have found a way to prevent potential tragedy and achieve resolution, explored both real and imagined fears through play and talk, and experienced the power of empathic relationships for supporting social development and learning.

Conclusion

In this chapter we have thought about play and talk as being similar in the ways that they can be encouraged to progress by sensitive adults. Adults play a key role in enriching the purposes that children have to use language and the challenge to find appropriate words and phrases to express what they want to say. This is done by using the child's ideas and intentions and by supporting and modelling language and attitudes.

Engaging in genuine discussions, listening and acting upon what children say and structuring open-ended playful situations for children to experiment with language will give practitioners valuable opportunities to learn about and record children's progress.

The notion of children having spaces in which to think and talk suggests different types of supporting strategies that give children encouragement to be creative in their language. Spaces refer not only to restful yet interesting environments but also to spaces in time to allow for creative thoughts and reflective consolidation to occur. The skilled business of intervention and interaction in children's play has significant implications for the creative spaces in children's minds.

POINTS FOR REFLECTION

Yourself

'Down-time' is considered essential to allow children opportunities to reflect on and consolidate their learning. Do you believe that enough time is built into each day for this to happen effectively?

Your practice

How could you encourage and plan for conversations with children which will extend their understanding?

References

Bruner, J. (1986) *Actual Minds, Possible Words*. Cambridge, Mass: Harvard University Press.

Chomsky, N. (1957) *Syntactic Structures*. The Hague: Mouton.

Clark, R. (1992) 'Principles and practice of CLA in the classroom', in N. Fairclough (ed.) *Critical Language of Awareness*. London: Longman.

Claxton, G. (1997) *Hare Brain, Tortoise Mind*. London: Fourth Estate.

Cox, B. (1998) *Literacy Is Not Enough*. Manchester: Manchester University Press and Book Trust.

DES (1990) *Starting with Quality* (Rumbold Report). London: DES.

DfES (1999) *All Our Futures*. London: DfES.

DfES (2000) *National Literacy Strategy*. London: DfES

DfES (2002) *Birth to Three Matters. Framework*. London: DfES.

DfES (2003a) *Excellence and Enjoyment: A National Primary Strategy*. London: DfES.

DfES (2003b) *Creative Partnerships*. London: DfES.

Eysenck, M.W. and Keane, M.T. (2000) *Cognitive Psychology*. Hove: Psychology Press.

Greene, J. and Coulson, M. (1995) *Language and Understanding*. Milton Keynes: Open University Press.

Holmes, J. (2001) *The Search for the Secure Base*. Hove: Brunner-Routledge.

Loveless, A. (2005) 'Thinking about creativity', in A. Wilson (ed.) *Creativity in Primary Education*. Exeter: Learning Matters.

Meek, M. (1988) *How Texts Teach What Readers Learn*. Bath: Thimble Press.

Nurse, A. (2001) 'A question of inclusion', in L. Abbott and C. Nutbrown (eds) *Experiencing Reggio Emilia*. Buckingham: Open University Press.

Pugh, G. (2001) *Contemporary Issues in the Early Years*. London: Paul Chapman Publishing.

Sylva, K., Melhuish, E., Sammons, P., Siraj-Blatchford, I., Taggart, B. and Elliot, K. (2003) *The Effective Provision of Preschool Education Project: Findings from the Preschool Period*. London: Institute of Education.

Vygotsky, L. (1962) *Thought and Language*. Cambridge, Mass: MIT Press.

Wells, G. (1986) *The Meaning Makers*. London: Heinemann.

Winnicott, D. (1971) *Playing and Reality*. London: Routledge.

CHAPTER 6

What children know and can do

- All children have abilities which should be identified and promoted.

- Get to know each child and have high expectations of them based on our knowledge of them. Social relationships are a vital part of learning.

Building on children's previous knowledge

All children have abilities which are unique to themselves. In any setting 'Teachers need to know about the progress of the children so that work can be adapted to meet their, often unpredictable, variety of needs' (Black and Wiliam 1998). If practitioners are to build on what children know and can do then it is important that their capabilities are identified so that the children's knowledge and understanding can be promoted and extended.

There are many ways in which practitioners can find out about their children's development, preferences and abilities and this chapter explores some of these. In it we discuss the place of assessment and the ways in which effective assessment can take place within the normal routine of the preschool setting through observation and listening to children. It also looks at how discussion with the individual child about his or her own learning not only gives the practitioner a better idea about how that child thinks but also allows the child to begin to think about and even assess their own learning.

The place of assessment

Most practitioners will know that assessment is important and indeed a require-ment within the early years setting and Reception class but the reasons why it is so important may not always be clear.

Mary Jane Drummond (1993) believes that 'It is the teacher's responsibility to check whether the world they invite Jason to inhabit as a pupil is the one that makes sense to him as a child' (p. 10). This a good starting point from which to explore the place of assessment in early years settings and one that perhaps has the most resonance for those of us working in the early years. For knowing the chil-dren in the setting are happy, well settled and progressing in their learning will help us to plan better for the development of individual children. Furthermore, knowing what the child understands and can do allows us to provide experiences which will match each child's cognitive development.

Added to this, an exploration of the differences in the ways in which individu-als and groups of children learn and an understanding of how they interact with each other and the adults will not only allow for the development of a curriculum and pedagogy suitable for our own setting but also help us to understand better the curriculum that already exists within it.

Young children learn by trying to make sense of their experiences all the time and their engagement with learning is holistic and is not compartmentalised by subject. This contextualised way of learning in the early years makes the logistics of carrying out assessments and recording the findings difficult, especially when we consider that all of the children need to be assessed.

Furthermore, according to Mary Jane Drummond (1993) the difficulties associ-ated with assessment are not merely pragmatic:

> Trying to understand the place of assessment in education makes moral and philo-sophical demands on our thinking. The practice of effective assessment requires a thorough understanding and acceptance of the concept of rights, responsibilities and power, lying at the heart of our work as teachers. In searching for ways to make our assessment practices more effective we are committing ourselves to recognising chil-dren's rights, shouldering our responsibilities towards them, and striving to use our power wisely and well.
>
> (Drummond 1993:11)

All of us have our own beliefs, values, ideas and opinions that shape the way in which we think, act, interpret and understand our field. These views, from which we develop our own ideologies and philosophies, will affect both the ways in which we carry out assessment and how we make sense of what we see and hear. To make the most of assessment opportunities we also need to be interested in investigating and finding out the answers to genuine questions and to under-stand our own motives for carrying out the assessment. There are a variety of

How children interact with each other

reasons why we might want to assess the children in our setting and some of these are included in this chapter.

Assessment to develop the curriculum

Managing and organising an early years setting is dependent in part on reviewing provision and using information gathered to plan the curriculum which is presented to the children. Effective assessment is essential if practitioners are to develop a curriculum which will provide the children with what they need in terms of their education and care. Assessment will provide a basis upon which the statutory curriculum is transformed into the actual curriculum that is offered to the children in practice. The intended learning outcomes planned by practitioners for activities or the sensitive interactions that take place during child-initiated play will be derived from the overall curriculum and the day-to-day assessment of the children's response. Assessment of children's responses has to be part of the planning if it is to be effective. So effective assessment relies on careful planning, and appropriate planning depends on assessment. The dependency of planning on assessment and assessment on planning is sometimes known as the assessment and planning cycle.

Assessment should not be seen as an add-on activity; rather, it should be integrated carefully into the normal routine of the setting. It is important that assess-

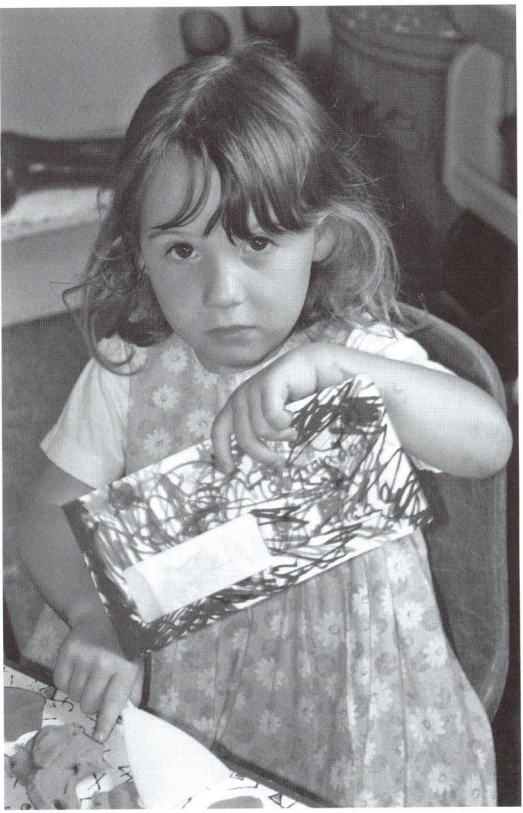

To evaluate their own work

ment arrangements are included at all levels of planning: at curriculum development level, within termly plans and within day-to-day plans.

Assessment within statutory requirements

There is a requirement in England for practitioners in school Reception classes to assess children's learning informally throughout their Reception year. This is ongoing assessment which ensures that by the end of the Foundation Stage (which coincides with the end of the children's Reception year) there will be a complete Foundation Stage profile for each child. Each child's development is expected to be assessed against the Early Learning Goals as laid out in the *Curriculum Guidance for the Foundation Stage* (QCA 2000). These profiles are used not just for the information for the teacher but also for reporting to parents and to the child's next teacher. Later, at the end of Key Stage 1, in England, along with teacher assessment, children are expected to take more formal tests and tasks for English and mathematics which contribute to the allocation of a level of achievement to each child. These levels are used not only for reporting to parents but also more universally for comparisons between different cohorts of children and to identify general areas for improvement of the school.

What we might assess

It is important to get to know children as individuals and the first assessment we might consider as a child enters the setting is to find out what the child already knows and understands.

Children will arrive at the preschool setting with a variety of outside school or nursery experiences and it is important for practitioners to take this into account, both giving it the status it deserves and using this wider understanding to contextualise new ideas. Many nurseries or preschool settings will ask parents to complete an entry questionnaire about their child's previous experiences. This kind of activity not only gives parents the opportunity to share their perspective on their child's development, it can also help practitioners to build good relationships with the parents as they will value the respect shown for their knowledge of the child. Parents' responses can give a good insight into the child's early home and other experiences which can be looked at alongside any early observations carried out in the setting. Practitioners can also gain a sense of what has gone before by observing the child in question and by listening to what he or she says. The knowledge gained from both of these activities can be used to plan a suitable curriculum for the child, which will take account of their prior knowledge, preferred learning styles and interests.

For example, after talking to Maria's parents it was clear to the nursery nurse that one of three-year-old Maria's main interests was role play and acting out familiar stories. The practitioner was able to ensure that, in her early days within the setting, Maria was able to choose to play in the play house if she so wished by making sure that the other children were amenable to allowing her in. Maria quickly established herself as a member of the group and was soon seen to be directing the other children to play Cinderella ('I'll be the princess and you can be the fairy Godmother').

Settling into the setting

Practitioners can use assessment to find out how children are settling in to their new situation and how well they are coping with separation from their parents. Much information about the child's well-being can be gained by observing the child at play both inside and outside. By watching the child the practitioner can find out, for example, how he or she spends time, whether he or she plays alone or in a group, who he or she plays with, what he or she enjoys and worries about.

Tim had recently joined the Reception class and Jane his teacher decided to observe him at timed intervals over the course of half an hour to find out how he was settling in. In her notes she recorded that throughout the session he played alone. He first chose to 'play fight' with some small farm animals, in a model farm, and then to sort the animals into groups and place them in a variety of visually symmetrical or repeating patterns. He played on the computer. From this observation and from information that she had received from Tim's parents she realised that Tim was mimicking the types of activities his mother had said that he enjoyed at home. Tim seemed to be relaxed and happy within the activities he chose but Jane was a little concerned that he played alone. She decided that during the next session she would suggest to Avais and Joel, who had already been in school a term, that they might like to play with the farm alongside Tim. She hoped that this might encourage Tim to develop social relationships with others in a situation that was comfortable for him.

Relationships

Examining the number and nature of social relationships that children are developing can give the practitioner an insight into special friendships that are developing, difficulties children may have in relating to other members of the group and children who have become isolated. This type of assessment allows practitioners to deal with difficulties as they arise and before they become problematic. Practitioners may also want to explore how adult involvement and interaction affects both individual learning and the dynamics of any group with which they are working. Self- and peer-assessment of the responses of the adults within the setting to each other and the children and the children to the adults can be later used as a basis for staff development.

Children's learning

The most obvious reason for assessing children's learning is to find out whether the children are progressing in their learning, but assessment of learning can also give us an insight into the quality of a child's experiences, including the effectiveness of the teaching methods and pedagogical approach of the practitioner. Furthermore, by watching the learning process we can find out about the children's learning style preferences, discover how individual children are spending their time and build up a picture of the choices they make.

On-the-spot assessment which is focused on what the child can do also allows the practitioner to give support when necessary without allowing a dependency relationship to develop. Sensitivity to a child's understanding of any task will mean that a practitioner, through suitable dialogue and/or silence, can allow the child to evaluate their own work. By providing support for the child's search for meanings, tailored to the child's needs at a particular time, the adult ensures that the child remains in control of any activity in which they are engaged (Anning and Edwards 1999).

Choosing a method

It is important that practitioners choose a method of assessment carefully to suit both the purposes of assessment and the child being assessed. Highly skilled practitioners can 'select and use methods and techniques judiciously and inter-weave their judgements with child and primary carer dialogues to inform planning for children's future development' (Murray 2005).

One of the most commonly used methods in the early years to gather information to inform assessment is observation.

Observations

Carrying out observation of the children in your setting is a powerful way of judging children's attitudes and dispositions as well as what they know and can do and it is true to say that the more we watch the more we will see. 'Watching young children learn can open our eyes to the astonishing capacity of children to learn and shows us the crucial importance of these first few years in children's lives' (Nutbrown 2000).

When we observe children we are not only watching their learning we are also looking at the context in which that learning takes place. So that we can see, for example, what choices the child makes, the child's approach to a task and the interaction that takes place.

Observation is a key element to assessment particularly in the early years. The quality of observations made and the analysis that is drawn from them will determine the quality of assessment. Different people see different things and personal life and work histories will give each practitioner a unique set of values and beliefs. Interpretation of what has been seen, therefore, will depend on the experiences that the observer brings to the observation. This means that any single observation will be subjective. However, observing is probably the best chance we have to make sense of what the children are doing and why. Stepping back to think about whether we are interpreting a situation correctly, writing down what we see and hear, discussing our observations with other practitioners and comparing current and past observations will all help to give us a more objective approach over time.

It is clear that assessment can help us to understand the children that we are working with. If observation is considered to be an important form of data gathering for assessment then it must be planned as part of the day-to-day work of practitioners and time must be put aside for it. One way to make time in a busy preschool day for observation is to make the children as independent as possible. Practical solutions such as Velcro fastenings on aprons, sinks low enough for the children to reach and child-height storage can all aid independence. Children are often much more capable than we give them credit for and often enjoy the extra responsibility. Tasks such as washing up paint pots, which may seem mundane to us, may actually be quite exciting for a three- or four-year-old.

There are two main ways that observation can be carried out. The first is to observe as we are working with or talking to the children engaged in a particular activity. This participant observation is important and staff making notes as they work can build up very valuable records of the children's learning within such sessions. This way of observing will tend to give a narrow view of the child though, as the practitioner is usually guiding the children's choices and learning and consequently some areas of the children's development and learning may not be covered by this method. Recording from this type of observation will usually be on a focused assessment sheet (see 'Recording assessment' section below).

The second common form of observation is non-participant. This allows the practitioner to discover what the child can do when playing alone or with peers, how they interact with others and more generally what activities they choose to engage in. Staff in early years settings may be reluctant to engage in non-participant observation because they feel that 'doing nothing but observe' may be a waste of time. This is very definitely not the case because, as well as learning about the children as individuals, they can watch the setting in its entirety to explore any strengths and weaknesses of provision and to discover any issues surrounding the planned or unplanned curriculum. It can also give useful insights into areas such as behaviour, for example what triggers certain behaviour in the children or in the staff. There are a number of ways that observations of this sort can be carried out and recorded. One way is time sampling. This involves the observer in selecting an aspect of behaviour of one or more children and making notes every time the behaviour occurs. This would usually be on a tick sheet and note, for example, time and place, triggers to behaviour, length of behaviour and children involved. This can be later recorded on a graph so that patterns of responses can be determined. Sociograms and activity tracking charts are a useful method of recording children's social relationships, friendships and interaction with other children or adults in the setting or of developing an understanding of their interests and preferences (for an example see 'Recording assessment' section below). They can also be used to track the engagement of practitioners with children and activities as part of staff development.

There are a number of important points to bear in mind when observing children. It is more productive for planning if we follow the example of Athey (1990) at the Froebel Institute. She tried to look at children's development from a positive perspective. She built on Piaget's work in child development but rather than focus on what they could not do, as Piaget had done, she focused on what they could do. This positive way of assessing children helps us to develop strategies that facilitate children to build on the understandings they already have. We need to try to find a way to assess the process of learning, such as their strategies for solving problems, rather than the product. This is because unless we understand the way in which they learn we cannot hope to extend that learning. A 'can't do' approach will tell us nothing about how a child learns.

When making judgements about children's learning, welfare and development, it is important that the practitioners realise that differences in home culture will affect the children's responses to their preschool setting and that their previous experiences will, as ours, give them their own perspectives. It is therefore important, during observations, that we do not merely judge the children from our own viewpoint. If we are truly to understand what they know and understand, then we must try to see their perspective. Because of previous experience children often have different understandings, not wrong for them, as they may not have all the information that they need to come to an accepted conclusion.

We need to be careful not to put too rigid an interpretation on what children can and cannot do as some expectations are bound up in cultural expectation, perspectives and positions. For example, teachers and parents would be worried about a seven-year-old child in England who could not read, yet in other European countries such as Sweden and Finland no one would be worried because there is no expectation that children will read before they start school at seven.

Time given to observation can also have a positive effect on the development of practitioners' understanding of the theories of child development. Watching children at work and at play helps practitioners to clarify any understanding they may have of research in early education by theorists such as Froebel, Piaget, Vygotsky and Isaacs or by grounding in practice. This synthesis of the theory with practice will in turn put practitioners in a better position to consider their own observations in the light of the literature. This will help them to give meaning to the children's actions and responses.

Listening to children and asking questions

Listening to children talk and to the questions that they ask helps us to understand their learning. It is therefore important that children are encouraged to ask questions of each other and of the practitioner and to engage in discussion. Recording what children say can be part of the type of participant observation described in the previous section. Listening to what children say can also be part of non-participant observation, but in this case it should be remembered that the close proximity of the observer, that is necessary to hear what is being said, might affect children's responses. They may act differently in the presence of an adult than might otherwise have been the case.

Both listening to children talk and practitioners asking questions can give insights into the children's knowledge, understanding, thinking and preferred ways of approaching an activity, task or play situation. Open questions are usually the most effective in encouraging discussion and can also be used to challenge the children's thinking. However, framing the questions to illicit the information that we need is often difficult and we need to try to avoid putting words into the child's mouth. We also need to remember that while asking questions and listening to the answers can be a powerful way of assessing young children, care must be taken not to disrupt the child's play or to cross-question to the extent of making the child feel uncomfortable.

Questioning children is not always as easy as it seems and the practitioner needs not only to be sensitive to the child's moods and feelings but also to be open-minded enough not only to see the child's learning related to a particular concept but also to know more about the whole picture, such as the emotional dimension of learning and the child's dispositions towards learning.

Children's involvement in assessment

It is beneficial for children to become involved in their own assessment as this encourages them to think about what they are learning. It also helps them to analyse their own understanding, celebrate successes and become autonomous learners. Children's participation in their own assessment can give us an insight into their opinions, interests and preferred ways of learning. It can help us to better understand the child's perspective. Having an improved understanding of what motivates the child can also assist us in developing appropriate plans for the child's future development.

One way in which children can take part in their own assessment is by being asked to make decisions about the quality of their own work. This can include choosing examples to save in a learning journal or portfolio and giving reasons for their choices. In this way not only can children say what they like and why they like it, they will also have a record of their work that they can look back at to see their own progress. They can also share their successes with other children, practitioners or parents. Work that is saved does not always have to be in a written or paper based form as there are many other opportunities that can be used for developing personal records for the child. Children can be asked to take digital photographs, for example, of play situations or activities that they have particularly enjoyed or of models they have made, and to talk about why they have made the choice. Alternatively they can be encouraged to ask for photographs to be taken of their work. Other possible ways for children to record their own learning include the use of video or audio taping.

Encouraging children to be involved in their own assessment can give the children some ownership over their own learning. It can have a positive impact on their self-image, self-esteem, attitudes to learning and self-confidence as they are able to explain to the adult what particular aspects of their learning they are proud of and why (Ackers 1994).

Use of collected data

The evidence from practitioners' observations of the children can be used either to fine-tune the practitioner's response immediately or to contribute to the planning for subsequent learning to ensure that the needs of all children are met. It is important for observations and other assessments to be recorded carefully as it is these written comments that provide a record of child's experiences that will allow practitioners to look back at children's responses. Effective interpretation of practitioners' observations and other records in the longer term relies on practitioners having time to reflect on what they see and hear to make sense of the how and the why.

Written records that practitioners can draw on to inform their assessments may include interaction tracking sheets, checklists, profile sheets, focused assessment sheets (see following section for examples of these), summaries of children's achievements and transcripts of conversations. As well as being used for internal purposes, such as short- and long-term planning and staff development, these records can also be used as part of the evidence base that a setting needs to satisfy outside agencies such as Ofsted. Other data that can be collected as evidence of children's learning can include drawings, models, early writing, tapes of children talking, photographs and even video. It is also beneficial to include summaries of children's achievements, completed regularly, which draw on information from other data-gathering methods

Plans within a setting should be reliant on assessment and should be reactive to the particular class or group to which they refer. There are several levels of planning that are informed by the assessments that practitioners make, including immediate reaction to the situation, short-term plans, planning for the medium term or deciding what would benefit the children's learning in the longer term.

Experienced practitioners are able to assess children on the spot in order to support their development. This type of reactive assessment is important to the children's day-to-day welfare and learning. Furthermore, practitioners need to be perceptive to each child's capabilities if they are to successfully scaffold the children's learning appropriately.

Ongoing and informal assessment can also form part of a longer-term view and these informal assessments, if written down, can be used alongside more formal assessments to take stock of each child's development on a monthly or half-termly basis, as well as to take an overview to adjust the longer-term plans for the setting to suit the more immediate or medium-term situation.

One further use for practitioner assessment is to inform the children of their progress both in social terms and in terms of their learning. It is important that children are given feedback, even at a young age, so that they are encouraged and have a positive view of their own development. We need to build a success or 'can do' culture where efforts are discussed, problems are acknowledged and worked through and children are clear about how they might develop their own attitudes, dispositions and learning.

Recording assessment

Observation of children can take a variety of forms. One of the methods of assessment discussed in this chapter was time sampling. Observation notes from this can be converted into a graph, which can be used to help the practitioner spot patterns of behaviour that may give an insight into the reasons for the behaviour seen. Calum, for example, was prone to outbursts of temper. Staff could not determine a pattern to this behaviour until they carried out time sampling and converted this to a graph (see Figure 6.1). It was clear from this that the particular problem days were Monday, Tuesday and sometimes Friday. Staff thought at first

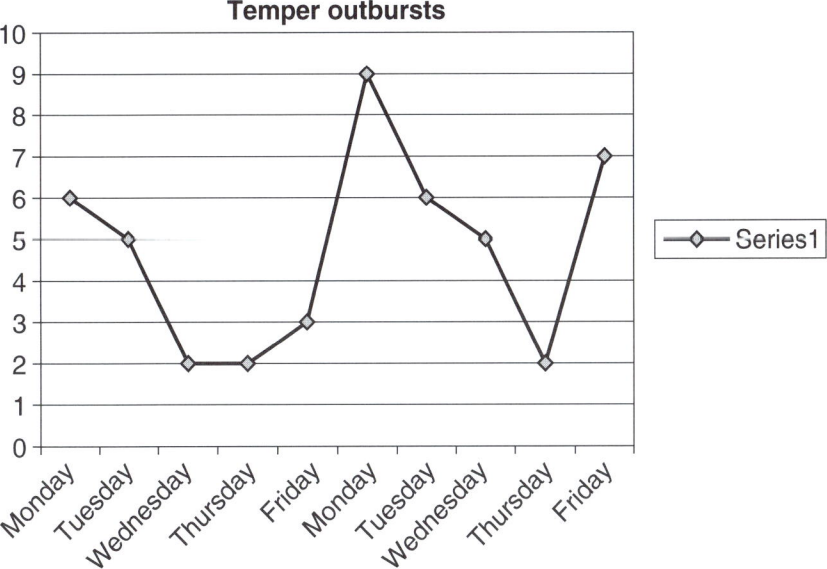

Figure 6.1 Temper outburst chart

that this might be linked in some way to what was happening over the weekend. On closer inspection of their notes and attendance records, however, they realised that most altercations were between Calum and Tim. On the days that Tim did not attend Calum appeared to be calmer. Staff decided on the basis of this to carry out a more in-depth observation of the two boys to determine the nature of the problem.

Another way to record non-participant observation is with the use of a tracking sheet. Below are examples of two types of sheet that may be used. The first sheet (see Figure 6.2) was used to record each movement of Amy. Staff were concerned that Amy was flitting from one area of the setting to another and was engaging only superficially with the activities provided. They decided that one of them should watch Amy for twenty minutes and complete a tracking sheet.

Analysis of the sheet once completed enabled practitioners to see the choices that Amy had made. As can be seen, the resulting chart indicated that while Amy did tend to move from one area to another she showed some preference for the play house. On further observation practitioners realised that Amy was using the other areas as an extension of her role play.

Sociograms can be used to record interactions between staff and children or between children and children. As part of their staff development, staff decided to observe each other to find out how they interacted with the children during child-initiated play. Take a look at the two charts in Figure 6.3 and 6.4 and try to decide on the style of each of the two practitioners.

Where the intention is to observe children as a participant observer, then the child's responses (including what he or she says) can be recorded on a simple pro-forma, as in Figure 6.5.

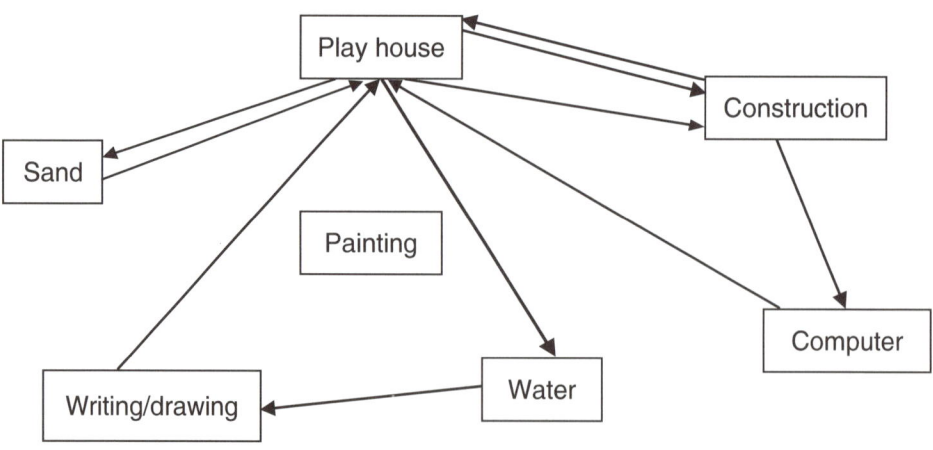

Figure 6.2 Movement tracking chart

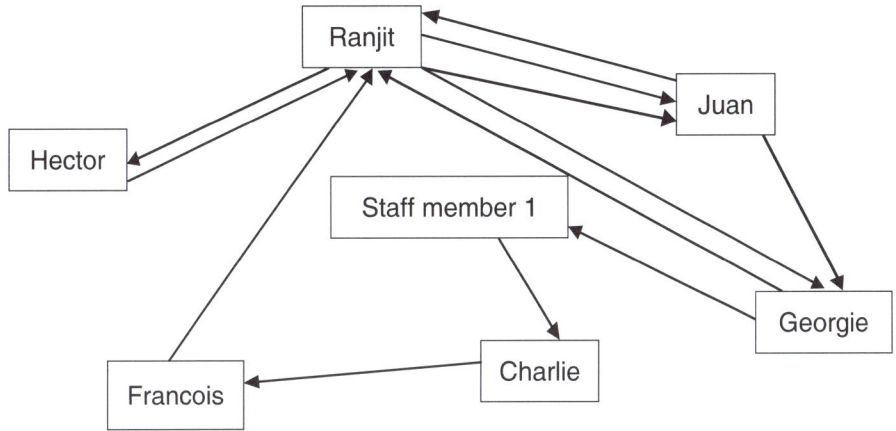

Figure 6.3 Sociogram version 1

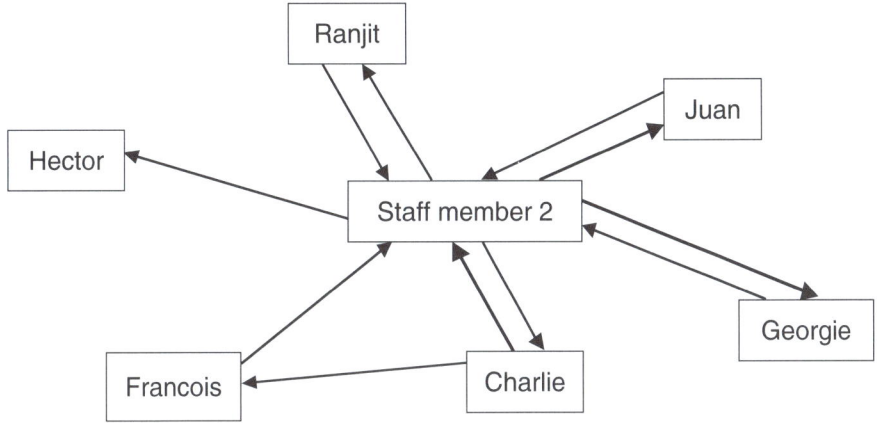

Figure 6.4 Sociogram version 2

Sometimes, where a firmer intended learning outcome has been set, perhaps for a playful activity, a practitioner engaged in participant observation with a group may complete an assessment sheet similar to that shown in Figure 6.6.

Children who are involved in their own assessment may complete a sheet with the help of a practitioner showing why they chose a particular piece of work to be included in their learning journal or portfolio. This is illustrated in Figure 6.7.

These sheets are, of course, just a small example of those which may be used and many settings will have their own methods of recording assessments. Before using any of the examples given above, the purposes of the assessments need to be decided in order to choose the most suitable recording sheet for the purpose.

Profile sheet

Date ....

Name ....

Figure 6.5 Profile sheet

Focused assessment sheet

Date..................

Intended learning outcome

....

Name	Comment

Figure 6.6 Focused assessment sheet

Name: James

Date: 21/10/2005

I chose this to include in my learning journal because:

I wanted to put this picture of me making this Duplo train because it is a

a long train and it can go round the room without the carriages falling off.

Practitioner's remarks:

James had been trying to join the Duplo together so that the pieces locked together for some days – his sense of satisfaction when he had achieved this was great. He showed several members of staff. He later used his new learning about how Duplo fits together to build what he described as a long lorry for cars.

Figure 6.7 Self-assessment sheet

Conclusion

The ways in which we gather information about children to inform us as to their future learning needs are crucial if we are to gain a holistic picture of their achievements. National outcomes for learning tend to lead practitioners to ask closed questions in order to tick boxes which can be isolated from everyday activities.

Research shows us that children give us higher scores if they are assessed during normal playful activities when they are unstressed and particularly if they are engaged in child-initiated play. We should also question what it is that we want to know about children. Is it only their academic progress that needs monitoring or should we also be interested in their life skills, such as their abilities to co-operate, communicate, persist, problem-solve and seek help?

Very young children should take an active part in recording their own progress. The scrapbook or learning journal plays a key part in valuing children's own views of who they are in the context of the early years setting.

POINTS FOR REFLECTION

Yourself

If you feel that the effort you put into assessment is wasted, what changes in the way assessment is applied would make you feel that it was worthwhile?

Your practice

How might early years children become involved in their assessment? What benefits would this have for their learning?

References

Ackers, J. (1994) 'Why involve me?: encouraging children and their parents to participate in the assessment process', in L. Abbott and R. Roger (eds) *Quality Education in the Early Years*. Buckingham: Open University Press.

Anning, A. and Edwards, A. (1999) *Promoting Children's Learning from Birth to Five: Developing the New Early Years Professional*. Buckingham: Open University Press.

Athey, C. (1990) *Extending Thought in Young Children: A Parent-Teacher Partnership*. London: Paul Chapman Publishing.

Black, P. and Wiliam, D. (1998) *Inside the Black Box*. London: NFER Nelson.

Drummond, M.J. (1993) *Assessing Children's Learning*. London: David Fulton Publishers.

Murray, J. (2005) 'Studying children', in T. Waller (ed.) *An Introduction to Early Childhood*. London: Paul Chapman Publishing.

Nutbrown, C. (2000) 'Watching and learning: the tools of assessment', in G. Pugh (ed.) *Contemporary Issues in the Early Years*. London: Paul Chapman Publishing.

QCA (2000) *Curriculum Guidance for the Foundation Stage*. London: QCA.

CHAPTER 7

Children learn at different rates and in different ways

- Children develop at different rates and in different ways.

- Respect the diversity of children's experiences and celebrate the richness that these differences offer the setting and the community.

Difference

This chapter is about difference. It will focus on the different rates and the different ways in which children learn. At times, particularly when discussing inclusive education, the word 'diversity' may be used in the same way as 'difference'. Practitioners knowing how to apply and make creative use of these differences will effect quality learning experiences for all the children in their care.

Differences can be broken down into three broad areas. The first shows the differences between assumptions of knowledge (or knowing). These inform many different values, beliefs or ideologies about teaching and learning. Current practice relies on two theoretical strands of knowing. These relate to knowledge as being objective and external to the human condition, and knowing seen as being subject to internal human process in constant interaction with the environment. This is how ideas and values, or ideologies and philosophies, inform the way we think about the practice in early years settings.

Secondly, having identified the underpinning philosophy of early years practice, this chapter explores aspects of developmental and social constructivist theories of learning that help understand different *rates* and *ways* of development. It explores how curriculum content and pedagogy can simultaneously work to

Gateway of the senses

support differences in children's learning from a developmental, psychological perspective.

The third area considers how this is combined with socio-cultural diversity which can be used as creative opportunities for inclusion in the early years setting. In this way we will explore difference from a socio-cultural stance.

Looking at these differences will pull together the philosophical roots and psychological values that together will steer us towards a socially inclusive future. However, to move forward, we sometimes need to look back; so we begin with some education history.

Rationalism

Athey (1990) reminds us, '. . . as an epistemologist, Piaget asked questions central to education such as "what is knowledge?" . . . and "how do we come to know?"' The nature of knowing, or 'epistemology', has fascinated philosophers, educators and scientists since the ancient Greeks. For the purpose of talking about teaching and learning, epistemology attempts to explain 'How is knowledge transmitted?'

In the sand pit

or 'How do we learn?' Athey also reminds us of the difference between a practitioner's 'know-how' experience of working with young children, and a 'know why?' consciousness associated with professional progress (p. 31). A grasp of the epistemological roots of our practice will help us make sense of the principles inherent in sound beginnings. It will also help us to answer the 'why' questions in ways that are both personally and professionally empowering.

For the philosopher Plato, there was a very clear hierarchy of knowledge. Philosophy as the most abstract form was considered to be at the summit, descending to the most literal and practical, attributable to those tilling the land. This sense of hierarchy, which remains at the heart of Western thinking, often leads to different cultures, classes and, in the educational context, different curricula.

Identifying and differentiating valuable high status knowledge throughout the education system has been central to curriculum debate in this country from university to nursery, for many years. Hirst (1975) supports a rationalist, classical view when he says, 'If the acquisition of certain fundamental elements of knowledge is necessary to the achievement of a rational mind in some particular respect, then there at any rate cannot but be universal objectives for the curriculum' (p. 12).

Gardner (1993) believes we suffer from three 'biases' in our society. He calls them Westist, Bestist and Testist. ' "Westist" involves putting certain Western cultural values, which date back to Socrates, on a pedestal. Logical thinking, for example, is important; rationality is important; but they are not the only virtues.' Foreseeing the need for broader definitions of intelligence and curriculum, he criticises our emphasis on logical thinking and rationality dating from classical times.

Mass education began comparatively recently, in the 1860s. Like the rest of society it was ordered from the top, down. The top was represented by a social and academic elite in the form of a public school system that produced influential people who would perpetuate a secure and stable, established structure. The concept of the grammar school has been described as a watered-down version of this system.

Gardner's third bias is 'Testist'. ' "Testist" suggests a bias towards focusing on human abilities or approaches that are readily testable. If it can't be tested, it sometimes seems, it is not worth paying attention to' (Gardner 1993). At the same time, the rise in public examinations (Maclure 1968) helped maintain the role of a new elementary school curriculum as being the narrow task of preparing children for grammar school. Achieving a grammar school place hinged on tests designed to measure intellectual ability, or intelligence tests, such as the IQ test pioneered by Binet in 1905. This is still the case, of course, in some parts of England. Thus the elite minority were in a position to decide what was to be taught to the majority who found themselves at the bottom of the ladder. In elementary schools (subsequently primary) some reading, writing and arithmetic were taught as a means to an end. Thus, deep-seated power relations in schools were set. Practitioners awaiting a coherent, cohesive, unifying strategy for pre-school education (Pugh 1992) that does not reinforce this top-down thinking may find this influence challenging, particularly as the residual influences of these hierarchies of knowing (Kelly 1986) continue to attribute high social and educational status to objective bodies of knowledge. These external 'bodies of knowledge' manifest themselves as the discrete curriculum subjects, the content-driven teaching, learning and assessment methods in schools today that early years educators have consistently fought to resist.

Romanticism and children's development

John Locke (1632–1704) believed children were born as innocent 'blank slates' and that knowing is acquired through experience. Hume's (1711–36) belief was that we acquire knowledge through the gateway of the senses (Golby et al. 1975). The combination of these philosophies marked the gradual shift of knowing from outside to inside the child and so sense derived knowledge or empiricism became the building block of science. Thus objective, positivist, generalisable knowledge about the world was pursued through observation and experimentation (Pring 2000). It also provided a reaction against an earlier world view of a 'God-ruled static cosmos' (Slee and Shute 2003). However, the philosopher Rousseau (1712–78) contributed an alternative view. His view took into consideration the development and growth of Locke's virtuous child, shaped by the environment. This became central to the ideals of Romanticism given impetus by the Romantic poets' lament for nature and a rural idyll. Quinton (1996) provides a useful summary of Romanticism:

> The Romantic is said to favour the concrete over the abstract, variety over uniformity, the infinite over the finite, nature over culture, convention and artifice; the organic over the mechanical, freedom over constraint, rules and limitation, imagination to common sense, intuition to intellect.
>
> (Quinton 1996: 778)

In his famous novel *Emile* (1762) Rousseau epitomised the way Romantic individualism and relative, rather than absolute, values began to influence education. *Emile* offered a philosophy that saw children as innocent, different from adults and vulnerable to the corrupt influences of society. For Rousseau, learning was determined by understanding an individual's nature at each stage of development. He wrote: 'Every mind has its own form' (Boyd 1956). He also emphasised the power of the environment in determining the success of educational encounters as vital. This very different view of 'knowing', which emphasises starting from the subjective, developing world of the individual, has significant implications for teaching and learning, and is one that is more familiar to early years practitioners' 'bottom-up' perspectives.

Until Piaget, Darwin's evolutionary theories were the only source of insight into children's development. Piaget's interest began when he worked on the first intelligence tests for Alfred Binet in Paris. While the tests focused on children's correct answers, Piaget was interested in the wrong answers systematically given by children that led him to discern some underlying developmental consistencies (Light and Oates, in Roth 1990).

His research stemmed from observations of his own children and investigates the cognitive development of the individual child. While his work has been criticised for giving little consideration to social learning and the central cognitive function of language, his ideas about 'discovery learning', 'learning by doing' and 'learning through play' have permeated early educational settings since the 1960s. Piaget's model of intellectual development contributed key concepts that can help us understand the *rates* and *ways* in which children develop.

For Piaget, key concepts such as 'object permanence', 'centration', 'egocentrism' and 'representation' describe the child's journey towards abstract thinking and define internal mechanisms for learning and intellectual growth. Being able to make mental representations of physical actions and responses is particularly significant to concept formation, cognitive development and learning. Piaget describes the infant's earliest, sensory interactions with the world, such as sucking and grasping, as an organised sequence of repeatable behaviours called 'schemas'. Through continuous interaction with their environment the child builds on these schemas or 'threads of thinking' (Nutbrown 1994) until they become internal mental representations, automatically retrievable from the child's memory. This denotes the onset of symbolisation and concept formation that is the child's level of knowing. (See discussion on schemas as they relate to children's play in early years settings in Chapter 2.)

Piaget's theory of the three stages of development suggests that schema formation takes place from birth; this is the 'sensori-motor' stage. Between the ages of two and six years, at what he describes as the 'pre-operational stage', the child's mental representations are developing but will still operate at a schematic, physical level closely connected to physical interaction with the environment. The child will be at this crucial level of developmental thought while attending early years settings. Early childhood educators such as Nutbrown (1994), Athey (1990) and Fisher (1996) have written about how practitioners can support individual children by identifying their early action schemas and by actively engaging with the child's thinking through talk and play. Schemas 'are a way of understanding the learning behaviours of children' (Bruce 1991).

Daisy, at 14 months, is excited by the concept of 'up and down'. She has just learned to walk, and stands and sits using the words 'up' and 'down' as appropriate. She is always pointing to the sky and saying 'moon' and her favourite songs are 'Twinkle, twinkle, little star' and 'The grand old duke of York'.

Piaget suggests that processes contribute to concept formation. These might be schemas or representation, where activities are represented symbolically or through art, movement, dance or drama. Processes affect the following internal mechanisms that trigger intellectual growth:

- **Assimilation**: the taking in and matching of new information to existing knowledge.
- **Accommodation**: the point of growth or development when mental adaptation takes place.
- **Intrinsic motivation**: Piaget believed that the existence of a schema in a child's resource bank of actions itself created a motivation for its use that denotes a motive intrinsic to the schema.

For Piaget, 'match' and motivation are central to thinking about the relationship between assimilation and accommodation and intrinsic motivation. However, Vygotsky might argue that problem solving is a shared, social activity requiring a degree of 'mis-match' if the new learner is to maximise their 'zone of proximal development' (Slee and Shute 2003). Fisher (1996) writes:

'A child is ready to learn when his or her cognitive disposition and what is to be taught is matched.'

Katz (1993) describes a disposition as a tendency to 'frequently consciously and voluntarily exhibit a pattern of behaviour towards a broad goal'. This kind of tendency is intrinsically bound to the child's sense of who they are, what they have experienced and what they feel they are able to do. As children of different genders, and from different ethnic, social and cultural backgrounds, exhibit different dispositions, the practitioner needs to observe, learn and build this into their planning for match. It is important to keep in mind how closely embedded the child's social and emotional experience is in relation to their intellectual growth.

When Sam ran straight towards the new sandpit in the courtyard for the first time in late November, he recognised the yellow grainy stuff by recalling and associating internalised experiences which came from being at the seaside with his family. The first thing Sam did on this bitterly cold morning was to take off his coat, sit and pull off his shoes and socks before jumping into the sand because that is what he did on the beach. During this assimilation process, he was intrinsically motivated towards something he had previously experienced and enjoyed, but the context was unfamiliar, different from his summertime experience. To accommodate the exploratory learning potential of this decontextualised winter sandpit in a way that would develop his existing schema or mental representation, Sam was required to adapt to this new experience. Understanding the way these thought processes work can give an observing practitioner opportunities to plan for Sam's progression. Also it will help them to create challenging play activities that will match and extend the child's level of thinking. By focusing on an individual's intellectual stage, rather than their age, practitioners give themselves the opportunity to monitor, assess and develop the child's cognitive progression, in ways compatible with those of Dewey.

John Dewey was the reconstructionist who consolidated Romantic ideals by introducing progressivist values; these really struck at the core of a system that traditionally aspired to initiating children into the knowledge and values of received culture. Progressivist is a term that continues to provoke fear and anger in rationalists as it mistakenly became synonymous with misgivings about 'child-centred' education in the last twenty years of the twentieth century.

Dewey saw knowledge as hypothetical and subject to constant change, modification and evolution. Passionate about independent thinking, he saw children as decision-makers and natural problem solvers in a constant state of interaction with their changing environment. For Dewey, the criteria for evaluating one set of activities (or curriculum) and experiences against another were to assess the extent to which each is progressive in terms of experience and development. In this way knowing is constantly being reconstructed through continuous, developmental experiential learning, and it places the child as a life-long learner at the heart of the process. This also has implications for attempting to measure intelligence in definitive ways by testing, as it can be seen more broadly as applied knowing, rather than the sum of any particular form of knowledge. Constructivists value children's experience as the starting point for developing or constructing new ideas, rather than assuming there is an absence of knowledge for the teacher to fill. De Boo (2004), Bruner and Vygotsky saw a much more prominent role for the teacher in bridging or 'scaffolding' (Fisher 1996; Whitebread 1996; Nutbrown 1994) children's understanding between existing and new skills and knowledge.

Stephen is trying to cut a piece of paper using a pair of scissors. At first his co-ordination is not well developed enough to hold the paper with one hand and the scissors with the other. The practitioner offers to help by holding the piece of paper and enabling Stephen to concentrate his abilities on using the scissors. In this way Stephen retains ownership of the task and can feel pride in his success.

Thus it is the interaction between Stephen and his teacher that becomes central to knowing and extending learning. Unlike the 'child-centredness' associated with Romanticism or rationalist epistemology associated with objectifying knowledge, social constructivists such as Vygotsky and Bruner offer a more dialectical approach. This viewpoint offers a different starting place for thinking about curriculum and pedagogy.

Curriculum and pedagogy

Gardner (1993) particularly challenges the traditional, narrow view of intelligence and intelligence testing. He also underlines the different priorities of top-down and bottom-up thinking when he describes a one-dimensional 'uniform' school where the curriculum is imposed; where there are a set of facts to be learned and where children with higher IQs proceed to higher ranking schools, universities and possibly lives. This 'uniform approach' does not account for the intellectual, social and emotional lives of children. Nor does it account for individual motivation, dispositions, or the multiple intelligences Gardner identifies.

Gardner sees a pluralistic rather than hierarchical view of knowing, and, like Dewey, Piaget and Bruner, is interested in practical problem solving. One of the assumptions his ideal school would rely on is that children do not have the same interests and abilities; nor do they all learn in the same way. Gardner's work can liberate practitioners who might otherwise be preoccupied with the demands of literacy and numeracy at the expense of nurturing a broad and balanced range of children's competencies. He suggests we all have different combinations of intelligence that we bring to bear when faced with different problems in different situations at different times. This, of course, multiplies the variables for the practitioner hoping to identify a child's preferred mode of learning, or learning style.

However, recent research by Coffield *et al.* (2004), questions how we use our understanding of learning styles. The research suggests that we ought to increase children's awareness of a range of possible learning styles and strategies they may have at their disposal. Children will then be in the independent position of choosing a style to fit the specific task in hand. These ideas imply that we should encourage children to be more aware of their own diverse strategies for learning, that is, to encourage thinking about thinking in a meta-cognitive way. In the early years setting this would be compatible with socio-constructivist values and practices realised through play, talk and shared sustained thinking.

As practitioners we cannot think about *rates* and *ways* of young children's learning unless we believe the way we teach affects that learning. It is difficult, then, to divorce development and learning from teaching because they are inextricably bound, or can be seen as two sides of the same coin. The way we teach, what we teach and why we teach it will depend on a wide range of interrelated, interdependent variables surrounding the development of the child, the environmental context and the curriculum.

The development of the child is holistic, but can be broken down into cognitive, physical and socio-emotional growth. Differences within and between children in all these areas will be vast. The environmental context will depend on the immediate cultural experience of the child within their family and community setting, which is inevitably informed by wider political and social issues. Differences here will also be vast. The curriculum in the early years setting will reflect either the beliefs and values of those in charge of the setting or, increasingly, the beliefs and values of the government in the form of the Foundation Stage Curriculum or the National Curriculum.

A reactionary political shift during the last twenty years of the twentieth century has positioned knowledge as a socio-economic commodity. This utilitarian approach has undermined the notion of educational philosophy and turned 'progressivism' into a pejorative term in mainstream schools and in society. However, Dewey's ideas, along with those of other significant early years thinkers such as Isaacs and Froebel, have been supported by empirical observations of developmental psychologists such as Piaget. These have been extended further by social constructivists such as Bruner and Vygotsky and enshrined in the curricula of New Zealand and Reggio Emilia. Given this multidiscipline approach, we can begin to see why such ideas have been integrated into the organic, holistic child-centred ethos of practitioners in early years settings who are interested in learning how children come to know and make sense of themselves in their environments.

Types of knowing that are valued are reflected in the content of the curriculum by breaking the curriculum into subjects. Part of the reasoning behind nationalising the curriculum was to ensure common subject content that would provide cohesion, continuity and accountability throughout schools in this country. However, this has led to a chronologically structured, outcome-driven system measured by statutory testing. Nowhere does this account for any of the developmental differences, either in the child or those generated by the increasingly complex, pluralistic and culturally diverse surroundings in which we find ourselves. In the 1980s, nationalisation was dissipated on the grounds that it levelled down and fostered mediocrity. Turning education into a nationalised industry during the same period, however, was evidently not equated with such an outcome.

The content of the curriculum and how it is taught is a problematic issue that continues to surround early education issues. A National Curriculum in mainstream schooling sets a strong precedent for early years settings to comply with a top-down model. The extensive content of an age-related National Curriculum specifically linked to learning objectives inherently influences methodology or pedagogy when it is described as 'both the behaviour of teaching and being able to talk about and reflect on teaching' (Moyles *et al.* 2002). Additionally, 'top-down' pressure to devise an early years curriculum is difficult to reconcile with government reports that acknowledged that the starting points for learning are seen as the needs and characteristics of the child. The 'Startright' Report (1994) gave impetus to this when Ball stated: 'Children develop at different rates, and in different ways – emotionally, intellectually, morally, socially, physically and spiritually. All are important; each is interwoven with others' (p. 51). However, *Desirable Outcomes for Learning* (Schools, Curriculum and Assessment Authority (SCAA) 1996) disappointed many practitioners by describing the shape of a syllabus that identified six areas for children's learning on entering school at four, with almost total avoidance of the word 'play'.

Following this, a group of early years organisations came together in 1998 to become the Early Childhood Education Forum, a coalition of interest groups including early years educators and parents. They devised *Quality in Diversity in Early Learning* (National Children's Bureau 1998). This is a framework to help early childhood practitioners consider, support and extend the learning of young children from birth to eight years. Influences included 'HighScope' (Hohmann *et al.* 1979) and Reggio Emilia (Edwards *et al.* 1993) and the SureStart project. But ideas were particularly drawn from the New Zealand's Maori Te Whariki curriculum model (Carr *et al.* 2000) which is culturally, philosophically and developmentally meaningful. This early years curriculum has four underpinning principles:

- empowerment
- holistic development
- family and community
- relationships.

The basis of this curriculum is very different from a long-term investment in subject knowledge. It is easy to be sidetracked by the seductive, socially inclusive emphasis of these principles, but it is important to remember that they, as those of Reggio, are culturally meaningful and therefore culturally specific. To ensure our pedagogic principles are equally inclusive and equally culturally relevant and specific, we need to construct our own. The transition we are faced with is that if every child's experience is seen as unique, we need to think beyond the biological development of the child. We need to think about the child's developmental interaction with the child's specific social and cultural context. Research shows that context affects cognition, socio-emotional and emotional well-being, educational achievement and life chances. Only by coming to terms with, engaging with and embracing the complexities of diversity politically, economically and socially can we begin to formulate aims and values in educational practice that will be as culturally meaningful as that demonstrated by Te Whariki and Reggio.

Taking account of difference requires flexibility, rather than adhering to fixed prescribed categories or classification of knowledge. We seem to yearn for certainty and consistency, and educational settings can often be the only secure, reliable base children experience. However, instead of investing in human consistency and understanding, we seem increasingly to invest materially in systems, structures and procedures that appear to organise and simplify but are not designed to include difference. When does classification, categorisation and labelling become stereotyping, and stereotyping become prejudice? It is difficult to begin to think about reconceptualising curriculum without acknowledging the deeply entrenched grip teaching subjects has, even with the youngest children in our care. As De Boo (2004) points out, children's learning does not occur in a linear or structured way to fit into shapes and categories we define. Whatever we do to stimulate and guide their learning, young children engage with and participate in what matters to them at the time, no matter how many tick boxes or objectives we have in mind. Selleck (2001) reminds us of how important it is to reflect on children's meanings and intentions before planning or making decisions about supporting the child's learning. A fixed curriculum and methodology may relieve practitioners of this uncertainty, but are we then depriving children of this space in our heads and therefore opportunities for quality learning experiences? So, can pedagogical principles be flexible? Can we bear pedagogical uncertainty? As Dewey (1933) pointed out: 'Nothing has brought pedagogical theory into greater dispute than the belief that it is identified with handing out to teachers recipes and models to be followed in teaching' (p. 170).

The Early Childhood Education Forum influenced the QCA Foundation Stage Curriculum (2000) which retained the six areas of learning identified in *Desirable Outcomes* (SCAA 1996) but emphasised the role of play and holistic learning in the early years.

The Study of Pedagogical Effectiveness in Early Learning (*SPEEL*) project (Moyles *et al.* 2002) worked on identifying components of effective pedagogy that are embedded in the practice of those working with children between the ages of three and five, including those at Foundation Stage in school.

The SPEEL researchers used 'reflective dialogue interviews' (p. 122) to capture the 'richest form of knowledge'. This they took to be the practitioner's own knowledge and understanding. This kind of knowing can be applied by the early years practitioner to each and every specific context (as with Stephen), where teacher–child interaction involves engaging with and reflecting on children's experiences, stage of development and learning needs, for example when observing, discussing and planning appropriate play experiences. The SPEEL researchers suggest this knowing, which they describe as 'pedagogical content knowledge', can be distinguished from and indeed 'transcends subject knowledge' (p. 122) by embracing the pedagogical processes that enable children to access learning.

A definition of 'effective pedagogy' is complex and difficult, but the SPEEL model embeds the teaching and learning curriculum within a broader interrelational concept of personal, cultural, care and community values:

> . . . both the behaviour of teaching and being able to talk about and reflect on teaching. Pedagogy in the early years operates from a shared frame of reference (a mutual learning encounter) between the practitioner, the young child and his/her family.
>
> (Moyles *et al.* 2002).

This prioritises and values a teaching and learning interaction that is different from transmitting curriculum subject knowledge as main objectives.

Inclusion

There is a tension between a curriculum outcome driven pedagogy and an early years practitioners' pedagogy of learning being developmentally and socially constructed. These tensions are currently exacerbated by the government's ideal of inclusive education.

Inclusion can be seen to be a multidimensional concept that may operate physically, cognitively and socio-emotionally in an interdependent way on many different levels. Thinking about inclusive issues in education can encourage us to interrogate our own assumptions concerning disability, ethnicity and gender as well as Special Educational Needs. Clough (2000) offers a useful overview of perspectives on educational inclusion, which traces five overlapping and interrelated phases from 1960s 'psycho-medical legacy' through to the 'disability studies critique' of the 2000s. The perceptions of disability represented by Acts favouring segregation (the 1899 and 1902 Education Acts) for 'mentally and physically defective' children, until the UNESCO (1996) idea of *all* children being educated in regular schools, indicates something of the slowly changing pace of attitudes and values associated with Special Educational Needs in our society.

However, the move away from what is described by researchers as a 'medical' model and the gradual journey towards a 'social' model is in process. This has been supported by a series of government Acts and educational legislation towards inclusion since the Salamanca Agreement (1994). As meanings are ascribed in words, a brief look at some of the language of inclusion and exclusion may help us to see the importance of celebrating diversity and working with young children towards breaking down barriers to learning.

Some of the thinking behind a 'medical' model of SEN may be revealed in its use of language. Terms such as 'invalid', 'victim of', 'afflicted by', 'suffering from', 'handicap' and 'mental' have negative connotations to the extent that the impairment or condition can become the focus of attention rather than the child as a person. Labels drawing attention to describing a child's disability may suggest there is something 'wrong' with the child that prevents them from functioning effectively. If this view is generally perpetuated it will put the child at a disadvantage within a mainstream setting, thus acting as a segregating, distancing mechanism that could be thought of as dehumanising.

Philip, aged four, is profoundly deaf. In his setting he is being encouraged to share one of his BSL signs each week with his peer group. He has taught them the signs for 'hello', 'goodbye', 'thank you' and 'please', thus becoming a contributor to the group. His friends enjoyed learning the signs and the process enabled Philip to feel a valued member of the group.

While the Warnock Report (DES 1978) recommended abolition of categories of handicap, it also established the concept of 'need', followed by a five-stage model of guidance (for LEAs, headteachers, governors and practitioners) in the form of the *SEN Code of Practice* (DfES 2001). This generated its own wide range of professional systems of intervention to support children and families. However, if a medical model perceives disability as a deficit and then constructs a whole system of SEN provisions to cure, tend, mend and 'normalise' the child, some form of labelling is bound to follow. Diagnosis, assessment, monitoring and programmes of therapy are part of the professional processes necessary for either reintegrating the child into a mainstream setting or in some cases excluding or segregating the child from mainstream into a special school setting. Also, some parents, overwhelmed by the SEN system and their child's difficulties, may welcome a label that helps them cope with feelings of grief and responsibility.

Rather than the impairment of the child, a 'social' model of disability identifies discrimination and prejudice in institutions with their policies, structures and environments as a principal reason for exclusion. It wants inclusion in society for all children as a basic human right and sees school as the catalyst for social change: 'The aim of "inclusion" is now at the heart of both education and social policy' (Mittler 1999). The language of inclusion carries key concepts such as 'support for diversity', 'breaking down barriers to learning' and 'access and participation for all' (Booth *et al.* 2004). A social model emphasises the need for more flexible systems so that school and teaching practices change to fit the child rather than the child to fit the system.

The idea of accepting and engaging with the child intellectually, emotionally, socially and physically is about practitioners considering the *rates* and *ways* in which children learn. Hornby (quoted in O'Brien 2002) illustrates this when he identifies four aspects of diversity or difference. These are:

- accepting and understanding
- using a range of teaching strategies
- range of placement and service strategies
- range of apt curricula options.

Accepting and understanding

Diversity relies on the practitioner engaging with and reflecting on each child's strengths and needs. It is about analysing a child's *rate* of learning.

Using a range of teaching strategies

This is about recognising individual children's stage of development. This is done by tuning into the child's intrinsic motivation and supporting schematic development and dispositions in order to structure and aptly bridge or 'scaffold' meaningful play, thus engaging with children in 'shared sustained thinking' (Sylva *et al.* 2002) in order to extend learning.

Range of placement and service delivery

Supporting children with additional needs may be facilitated by practitioners thinking holistically. Mittler (1999) says that recognising 'a society's values, beliefs and priorities will permeate the life and work of schools and does not stop at the school gate'. Actively working in a co-operative and collaborate way with parents, families and other professionals, both within and beyond the setting, supports the kind of inter-agency work underpinning the revised *SEN Code of Practice* (DfES 2004a). This is central to the government's *Every Child Matters* (DfES 2004b) agenda, and is a vital approach to creating inclusive cultures, practices and policies in early years settings.

Range of apt curricula options

This is essential in thinking about diversity. We need to consider how the curriculum we adopt addresses the *way* a child learns in the early years setting.

The National Children's Bureau asserts that apt content and the way in which it should be taught cannot be separated. They argue that 'the content derives from the method of working of practitioners and this should be defined and monitored within a framework (of which Quality in Diversity is an exemplar)' (NCB 2000). Corbett (2001) identifies curriculum rigidity as one of the negative forces at play in the inclusion debate and reminds us that attitudes and values, imbedded in principles and philosophies, help us to consider the interdependence of teaching and learning. He says, 'inclusive teaching is grounded in who you are as a person, your sense of worth and the contribution you make to the community now and in the future. It is also grounded in how you learn.'

Conclusion

Conflicting agendas lead to a confusion that can make it difficult for us to identify and hang on to the principles we believe in. Education is complex and multidisciplinary and has always been a fusion of scientific, psychological, philosophical and social enquiry. After another evening of teaching a group of disgruntled adult trainees, one teacher was told by an exasperated member of the group 'Look it's only teaching, you know; it isn't exactly rocket science!' Judith, the teacher, gave the memorable and profound response: 'No, you're absolutely right – it's far more complex than that!'

If we think knowing is built on the individual child's internalised experience and understanding of their continuing interaction with people and events in their environment, the practitioner's role will be just as much to do with their own capacity to learn about the child's interests, experiences and motivations. This together with what Katz (1994) describes as 'dispositions' should be the starting points for further development.

What we teach will depend on our observations of these things, including consideration of the individual's physical, socio-emotional and cognitive development. Understanding children's differences and meeting the needs of children will grow from the way we understand their similarities, and we will need to seek expertise from the child's parents and other practitioners or professionals to increase our own knowing and develop a community learning culture. This understanding will contextualise and inform the way we plan, interact with individuals, group and assess children so that the process of teaching and learning has a shared, internal validity and meaning for all those involved. The nature of this process will be about breaking down barriers to learning and supporting diversity.

In this chapter we have examined the different perspectives of how children learn. We have considered how principles for effective learning and teaching are developed from sound underpinning values and aims. Practitioners who talk about and reflect on teaching in the early years, who perceive engagement with children's different *ways* and *rates* of development as a mutual learning encounter (Moyles *et al.* 2002), will be working towards sound inclusive beginnings.

POINTS FOR REFLECTION

Yourself

The areas of the curriculum are not learned as discrete bodies of knowledge by young children.

Your practice

What ways are there to encourage a child's positive dispositions to learn? How can children be encouraged to build on their own preferred style of learning and any schematic play they have been observed doing?

References

Athey, C. (1990) *Extending Thought in Young Children*. London: Paul Chapman Publishing.

Ball, C. (1994) *The Importance of Early Learning* (Startright Report). London: Royal Society of Arts.

Booth, T., Ainscow, M. and Kingston, D. (2004) *Index for Inclusion: Developing Learning, Participating and Play in Early Years and Childcare*. Bristol: Centre for Studies on Inclusive Education.

Boyd, W. (1956) *Emile for Today*. London: Heinemann.

Bruce, T. (1991) *Time to Play in Early Years Education*. London: Hodder and Stoughton.

Carr, M., May, H., Podmore, V., Cubey, P., Hatherly, A. and Macartney, B. (2000) *Learning and Teaching Stories: Action Research on Evaluation in Early Childhood. Final Report to the Ministry of Education.* Wellington: New Zealand Council for Educational Research.

Clough, P. (2000) *Theories of Inclusive Education*. London: Paul Chapman Publishing.

Coffield, F., Mosely, D., Hall, E. and Ecclestone, K. (2004) *Should We Be Using Learning Styles?* London: Learning Skills Research Centre.

Corbett, J. (2001) *Supportive Inclusive Education*. London: Routledge Falmer.

De Boo, M. (2004) *The Early Years Handbook*. Sheffield: Geographical Association.

DES (1978) *Special Educational Needs* (Warnock Report). London: DES.

Dewey, J. (1933) *How We Think*. Levington, Mass: Heath.

DfES (2004a) *Revised Special Educational Needs Code of Practice*. London: DfES.

DfES (2004b) *Every Child Matters. Framework*. London: DfES.

Edwards, C., Gandini, L. and Forman, G. (1993) (eds) *The Hundred Languages of Children: The Reggio Emilia Approach to Early Childhood Education*. Norwood, NJ: Ablex Publishing Corporation.

Fisher, J. (1996) *Starting with the Child*. Buckingham: Open University Press.

Gardner, H. (1993) *Frames of Mind*. London: Fontana.

Golby, M., Greenwood, J. and West, W. (1975) *Curriculum Design*. London: Open University Press.

Hirst, P. (1975) 'Frames of mind', in M. Golby, J. Greenwood and W. West (eds) *Curriculum Design*. London: Open University Press.

Hohmann, H., Banet, B. and Weikart, D.P. (1979) *Young Children in Action: A Manual for Preschool Educators.* Ypsilanti, Mich: High/Scope Press.

Katz, L. (1993) *Definitions and Implications for Early Childhood Practices.* Urbana: ERIC.

Katz, L. (1994) *Reflections on the Reggio Emilia Approach.* Pennsylvania: ERIC.

Kelly, A. (1986) *Knowledge and Curriculum Planning.* London: Harper and Row.

Maclure, J. (1968) *Educational Documents: England and Wales 1816-1967.* London: Methuen.

Mittler, P. (1999) *Working towards Inclusive Education.* London: David Fulton Publishers.

Moyles, J., Adams, S. and Musgrove, A. (2002) *The Study of Pedagogical Effectiveness in Early Learning* (SPEEL). London: DfES.

National Children's Bureau (1998) *Quality in Diversity in Early Learning.* London: NCB.

National Children's Bureau (2000) Memorandum from the Early Child Education Forum, Local Authority Coordinators Network and Early Childhood Unit at the NCB (appendix 26. 3bvi, January).

Nutbrown, C. (1994) *Threads of Thinking.* London: Paul Chapman Publishing.

O'Brien, T. (2002) (ed.) *Blue Skies...Dark Clouds.* London: Optimus.

Pring, R. (2000) *Philosophy of Educational Research.* London: Continuum.

Pugh, G. (1992) (ed.) *Contemporary Issues in Education.* London: Paul Chapman Publishing.

Quinton, A. (1996) 'Philosophical romanticism', in T. Hondrich (ed.) *The Oxford Companion to Philosophy.* Oxford: Oxford University Press.

Roth, I. (1990) (ed.) *Introduction to Psychology.* Milton Keynes: Open University Press.

SCAA (1996) *Desirable Outcomes for Learning.* London: SCAA.

Selleck, D. (2001) 'Being under three years of age', in G. Pugh (ed.) *Contemporary Issues in Education.* London: Paul Chapman Publishing.

Slee, P. and Shute, R. (2003) *Child Development: Writing about Theories.* London: Arnold.

Sylva, K., Melhuish, E., Sammons, P., Siraj-Blatchford, I., Taggart, B. and Elliot, K. (2003) *The Effective Provision of Preschool Education Project: Findings from the Preschool Period.* London: Institute of Education.

UNESCO (1996) *Legislation Pertaining to Special Needs Education* (February).

Whitebread, D. (1996) *Teaching and Learning in the Early Years.* London: Routledge.

CHAPTER 8

Independence

- Children who are encouraged to act for themselves are more likely to act independently.

- Develop a setting where children can make choices and decisions. Encourage the development of their innate curiosity and of their ability to make sense of the world.

Introduction

Independence has a long and proud history in traditional early years practice in western Europe. For example, Friedrich Fröbel (1826) believed that 'the purpose of education is to encourage and guide man as a conscious, thinking and perceiving being'. The philosophy of the toddler and infant schools in Reggio Emilia is founded on the belief that a thinking, independent people will not easily submit to domination by political dictators. The belief in the right to independence of thought is enshrined in the United Nations Convention on the Rights of the Child (1989) where it is stated that 'You have the right to an opinion and for it to be listened to and taken seriously' (article 12). In most societies, as a child reaches adulthood they have to take many important decisions such as what job to train for, where to live, whom to live with and what to aim for. These decisions are easier to tackle if the individual has what is often called 'a strong sense of identity', a positive view of themselves as someone whose views matter and who, to some extent, can influence events in their lives. Sir Christopher Ball, in his outspoken report to the Royal Society of Arts in 1994, declared that, 'No-one learns effectively without motivation, social skills and confidence – and very few fail to learn successfully if they have developed these enabling attitudes and "super skills" of learning'. These powerful words suggest what we, as early years practitioners, have long believed. We believe that the 'what' (curriculum content) of teaching and learning is far less important than the 'how' (active, interactive and independent processes). Many successful leaders and entrepreneurs have not necessarily had high IQ ratings but have succeeded because of these 'super skills' of high motivation, self-esteem and good social interaction.

Independence, however, is a complex notion, particularly when it has to work effectively within an institution. It is hugely challenging for a large organisation such as a school to be responsive to individual and family needs and to ensure that all children 'are listened to and taken seriously'. It is here that time needs to be given to building effective relationships so that families have trust in the professionals and feel that what is important to them also matters to the school. Children's independence is hard to foster in a culture where 'children' need to become 'pupils' and adults' agendas, such as test results and success in numerical and literary skills and a compliant attitude in children, predominate. Children's independence and self-confidence may be challenged if they think in alternative ways to the expected norm or if they fail to understand the instructions and cultural mores of the institution they have joined. All early years professionals have stories to tell of the four-year-old who presents the adult with a dripping purple flower when asked to 'paint the crocus' and the child who looks bemused when asked to 'line up'. These are amusing illustrations of children who are yet to be fully integrated into the setting's routines and expectations and are small incidents which soon cease as the setting's requirements become more familiar. They do illustrate, however, that children enter settings as individuals and often have to accommodate their ideas and actions to those of the institution. For a fuller account of the need to embed institutional learning into children's home experiences see Margaret Donaldson's *Children's Minds* (1978).

Cognitive independence

As we have seen in preceding chapters, children's cognitive progression depends on their secure understanding of a wide range of concepts which need to be learned actively. Schematic play enables children to experience the 'coming to know' process with increasing confidence that their understanding is unassailable and that it can provide a firm foundation for new knowledge.

Children are competent learners well before they reach educational settings and already have strategies in place for assimilating new information. Their strategies depend on having a loving relationship with key carers, being able to ask questions that are important to them and being given time to consider the answers they receive. In the home environment it is the adult who usually responds to the child's lead and thus helps them to build a picture of themselves

Eager to talk about what they've done

as important, likeable and worthwhile. Successful progress towards cognitive independence is most likely if settings build on these strategies that families have put in place to support children and which children are confidently using (Bottle 2003). Sadly, settings sometimes find that these strategies are time-consuming and heavy on staffing so rarely lead immediately to the necessary outcome measures. If staff in all settings recognised that children's main access to knowledge is by talking and doing, then the command to 'sit down and be quiet' would be heard less often. This directive removes, at a stroke, children's main strategies for learning and often results in passive, compliant attitudes which, in turn, may lead to disaffection. Tizard and Hughes (1984), in their devastating study of working-class girls' home and school conversations, found that 'teachers were in no position to satisfy children's curiosity because the children hardly ever asked them questions'. This is clearly not the road to independence of thought.

With the introduction of *Birth to Three Matters* we will see more settings taking young babies. It is likely these will be the settings who are able, more skilfully, to fit their routines around individual preferences. The underpinning pedagogy of 'a strong child', 'a healthy child', 'a skilful communicator' and 'a competent learner' presents an image of already successful constructors of knowledge. The child's ideas, interests and patterns of learning should be extended and supported rather than manipulated to fit an adult need to progress in a uniform way through the stepping stones of achievement. It is this top-down model of instruction that takes from the young child the self-belief and confidence in their own abilities and leads to the loss of independent thought.

Required to listen to others

The practitioner who values children's self-belief understands their development sufficiently well to ask 'process' questions rather than 'naming' questions of, for example, a child's painting. The adult's comment, 'That's lovely, what is it?' is often unanswerable to a child who is exploring their understanding of how paint behaves or is practising mixing colours together. The process question, along the lines of 'Which bit did you do first?', is one that the child can answer and is usually only too pleased to discuss expansively! Similarly, the practice of issuing templates to encourage children's artistic abilities illustrates a belief that the adult's artistic representation is superior to the child's and that the child's is not worthy of consideration. Children asked to draw a house will often draw their bedroom as, to them, it is the most important room in their house. They will rarely draw the traditional square with the triangle on top and rectangles for doors and windows but will eventually do so if given enough templates, along with the message that their individual ideas are not worthwhile.

Making choices and taking ownership

If children have regular experiences of their ideas being worthy of adults' interest and attention, they will begin to build complexity into them by choosing how to progress or how to use that idea. At this point they are well on the way to what Carr *et al.* (2000) called 'taking responsibility' and Tina Bruce (1992) describes as 'free-flow play'. The key feature of this level of commitment to an idea is that it belongs to the child and it is they who have ownership of it. If children have ownership of ideas they are likely to be showing those aspects of effective learning that distinguish play from playing about. These aspects might be struggle, persistence, lengthy concentration and problem solving. The development of an internal locus of control can be thought of as a central element of becoming an independent learner, a learner who enjoys new challenges for their own sake and can risk the uncertainties involved in attempting something new. These children enjoy the intrinsic interest of something difficult rather than the need to gain the approval of an adult. Here may well lie the beginnings of a child's view of themselves as a 'mastery' or a 'helpless' learner which Kathy Sylva discussed in her research for the Startright Report (Ball 1994). Here she refers to the work of Carol Dweck, who investigated the aims of children attempting something new. Whereas most were orientated at points between a 'mastery' and a 'helpless' classification, some viewed the challenge of new learning as a test of their competence and 'needed to be judged by others as competent'. These she referred to as showing a 'helpless orientation' as they relied on an external locus of control and were motivated by the need to avoid displaying perceived inadequacies to others. Those showing this helpless classification often displayed a negative attitude to learning and deteriorating coping strategies. Children who, on the other hand, showed confidence and enthusiasm had acquired a realistic, though not necessarily over-positive, view of their abilities, and could match them to the attempted task. They seemed to believe that by effort and self-instruction they could achieve the task. Interestingly, Dweck claimed that this categorisation relies not on IQ measurement but on a view of oneself and ones' abilities. This would seem to echo Henry Ford's oft-quoted adage: 'If you think you can or if you think you can't, you are right.'

Making choices and taking ownership also involves the acceptance of responsibility for those choices. Herein lies a dilemma. In no other year groups are children offered the levels of responsibility that they are in the Foundation Stage. As we have suggested, the development of positive dispositions in young children leads towards autonomy and independence and yet it would also seem credible to suggest that in no other key stage are children so inexperienced and so dependent on adult support to progress academically, physically, socially and emotionally. Very young children are expected to choose what to spend their time doing, how long they will do it for and what the end result will be. They are required to be sociable, to share, to listen to others and to offer support and care for each other. They must also progress academically, particularly in numerical and literacy skills, and be able to make sense of their discoveries to connect pieces of new knowledge together. It can be a daunting prospect to turn an egocentric forty-eight-month-old child into an autonomous, independent problem solver!

Bennett *et al.* (1997), in their examination of the rhetoric and realities of teaching through play, highlighted the fact that many practitioners were not trained to teach children the skills that they need to begin their journey towards independence and some did not appreciate that these skills needed to be taught. This resulted in settings with very young children being given materials to play with in the assumption that independence would follow. Hoping that young children would always self-direct themselves could be thought of as an abdication of the adult's role. The teaching of specific skills targeted at helping children to make sense of their learning and to become increasingly independent is a crucial aspect of the setting's educational responsibility.

The role of the adult

So what skills do children need to maximise the opportunities offered to them in the rich and stimulating setting in which they find themselves? David Wood (1998) cites several attributes for which early years settings are renowned and some which may benefit from further consideration. He suggests that active learning helps children to 'encode' the material being handled and that, if active exploration is a regular way of learning, children can internalise and memorise the experience effectively. Memory is clearly a key requirement in the business of acquiring and building on new knowledge. It is important to realise that it is remembering an active experience (the 'learning how' that we considered in Chapter 2) that can be built on successfully. This is more helpful than memory as in rote learning (the 'learning that'). The *Curriculum Guidance for the Foundation Stage* (QCA 2000) is very clear that 'young children are active learners' and that 'learners need time to explore ideas and interests in depth'. These experiences will become the building blocks for progression.

Wood goes on to consider the child's ability to make sense of what they have learned. The process of helping a child to understand the significance of new knowledge, its links to existing knowledge and possible next steps, is clearly a big part of the practitioner's role. That is why it is vital for children to have regular opportunities to talk to a knowledgeable adult about what they have learned and how this learning fits into the context of what they know already and what they may learn next. This often happens during a small-group-time review as part of the 'plan, do, review' cycle and is instrumental in teaching those 'how to learn' skills.

Anna, the practitioner, had been with a group of three- to five-year-old children playing with water in the nursery garden. They had been experimenting with water which was poured through some overflow pipes. Anna asked Humza if he remembered which direction the water had taken. When he was unsure, his friend, Max, said, 'I remember, it went down, very very fast!' 'Do you think it always goes down?' asked Anna. A lively debate ensued at the end of which the children still remained doubtful as to the reliability of water to flow down on every occasion.

Anna re-enacted the experiment with a small tube and a jug of water as part of the group-time activity and was able to assess which children had learned the concept. This assessment led to her decision to plan more sessions of water pouring and to incorporate extension activities for those children who demonstrated that they had a secure grasp of the direction in which water flowed.[1]

The practitioner's role of extending learning is not always as straightforward. Christopher had spent nearly the whole morning session turning a cardboard box into a castle. When he showed it with pride to his key worker she attempted to extend his experience by suggesting he added a drawbridge with split pins and string. When he refused, saying it was finished, she offered her help and enthusiastically provided the materials they would need. Christopher stood watching, often looking out to the garden where his friends were playing, leaving the practitioner to complete the drawbridge. When Christopher was asked where he would like his castle to go now that it was finished he replied, rather sadly, 'I don't mind, it's your castle now'. The practitioner realised that, in the hopes of taking his learning further, what she had actually done, with the best of motives, was to remove the ownership of the castle from him. It is indeed a sensitive matter to balance the need to extend learning with that of understanding that enough has been learned at that point.

The practitioner had been very well intentioned. She had been trying to use Bruner's theory of scaffolding children's learning to help Christopher move on to the next stage. What she may have misunderstood is that scaffolding works well when a child has failed in their own eyes and is puzzled or confused as to how to progress. Then, the child knows that help is needed. In Christopher's case, he did not think he needed any help; his castle was finished and by being made to add the drawbridge (which was an idea in the practitioner's head and not in his) he had relinquished ownership of his work. Happily, this lesson was learned by the practitioner and children will only suffer if such attitudes predominate and become a regular occurrence.

The professional adult's role, then, is complex and varied. In the early years setting the word 'teaching' at some point will mean all of the following:

- listening
- enabling
- collaborating
- managing
- instructing
- observing

- extending
- assessing
- re-enforcing
- modelling
- mediating

1 This extract can be viewed in full on a DfES video called *Supporting Assessment for the Award of Qualified Teacher Status*, which was widely distributed to schools and teacher training institutions (Teacher Training Agency publication number 102/2–00).

Possibly one of the most effective roles for adults to take is that of modelling behaviour and language that children need to progress socially. The directive sometimes heard for children to 'play nicely' or to 'share' needs unpacking so that children are given strategies to get what they need in acceptable ways. By teaching children the words they will need to use, such as 'May I have that, please?', 'I haven't finished with it yet', or 'I'll give it to you when I've finished with it' will help them understand that words are more useful than aggressive actions. It needs monitoring, of course, by adults who have to support children who are not assertive enough to succeed in this method, but once the culture is established in a setting aggressive behaviour can be seen to diminish. Established children will teach new ones the words that are in common use and settings become calmer and more purposeful.

Similarly, children exhorted to 'be careful' rarely understand what danger they are about to encounter. Time needs to be found to explain that running may result in hurt children or spilled paint. If a request is phrased in a positive way – 'You need to walk in here' rather than the negative 'Stop running' – children will be more inclined to accept the directive and understand without any ambiguity what they have been asked to do. Clearly, if adults also model respectful and caring behaviour to each other, a powerful message goes to children as to the culture of the setting.

All of these roles involve an engagement with the child and a willingness to encourage them to make decisions and take responsibility. Drawing children into the planning process by asking their opinions of what they would like to learn about for a half-term project gives them genuine ownership of their learning. Similarly, making scrapbooks with leaving children which contain photographs they have chosen and scribed observations and opinions of things that are important to them, gives children the opportunity to take an active part in their own record keeping.

Possibly the role that leads to the most unease among practitioners is that of trying to join in with children's imaginative play. This is usually done to move on repetitive play and to offer the full range of opportunities that had been envisaged when the play was planned. Eve, one of the teachers in Bennett *et al.'s* research (1997), called this 'going in with your size tens' and accurately describes the fear sensitive adults have of trampling on and taking over young children's play. Most practitioners have at some point in their careers experienced that most humiliating of moments when their arrival in the home corner to join the tea party is greeted by a melting away of all the other players!

With practice, adults learn strategies that help them to become accepted in the role-play areas in their settings, but an understanding of principles is necessary before decisions are made about whether it is necessary to join in. What is the purpose of the interaction? Is it a negative interaction because the quality of the play is unacceptable? If so, are there other ways of raising the quality, such as altering the placing of the play, adding equipment or lengthening the time available to play? Sometimes children are unaware of how the area can be used and its full potential needs to be explained. Sometimes an adult needs to take the equipment, perhaps the appointment book or tickets, into a small-group time and model their use. Perhaps an adult can take a role at the start of a new role play. This seems to be a more acceptable strategy to children than the arrival of an adult once they have taken ownership of the game.

What is important when considering the adult's role in children's play is the recognition that the adult has important things to offer. In her research into early learning Kathy Sylva (Sylva *et al.* 2003) found that the consistent event characterising all good settings was what she called 'sustained shared thinking'. These are conversations, like the one Anna had with her children at group time about the direction in which water flows, which extend and challenge children's thinking, and where the learner and the teacher discover together, or 'co-construct', what is to be learned. Ideas may originate with the adult or the child but it must develop into a genuine partnership which contains mutual interest and respect. The nature of this partnership has implications for how adults see their role because if they spend their time continually doing up paint aprons or mopping up spilt water, they will not have time for conversations which need to be sustained and of intellectual worth. The solution to this dilemma is to organise the setting so that children can manage most of their own resources (including clearing up after themselves), leaving the adults free to talk to children about the content of their learning. This has the added advantage of demonstrating faith in the children that they can organise their own activities and helps them to develop independence.

A combination, then, of a stimulating environment and adults who know how to encourage children's independent thinking by skilful interaction will provide an environment where children will often surprise us, not only by the depth of their understanding, but by the creativity and responsibility of which they are capable.

Interdependence

Any discussion of independence should also consider that young children also need to function as *inter*dependent beings. In many ways this is a more complex notion than that of independence as it requires a child to be appropriately responsive to adults and peers. The truly independent child is not isolated but part of a complex network of social and emotional relationships spanning their whole environment, including both home and setting. The independent child sees themselves as a lovable, competent and strong person. This view is reflected in their ability to support more vulnerable children, accept help when they recognise that they need it and actively seek assistance from those they know can provide it. Practitioners need to know all their children well and organise learning so that children can work alone, in pairs or in friendship groups. They need to recognise that some children will be able to access all the facilities that are at their disposal easily, but that others will need gentle encouragement to build up enough trust to become genuinely interdependent. Interdependence requires a maturity of outlook which enables children to empathise with others and to see others' points of view. When this happens children can be said to have developed 'theory of mind', which is also when they begin to form firm friendships. They can become more vulnerable as it becomes apparent to them that their opinions are not necessarily those of everyone else, and they need to build resilience to rebuffs and failures. Because of children's different levels of maturity and their different personalities, children will vary widely in the amount and type of interdependence they seek.

David, aged nearly five, is a skilled model maker. He spent a long time in the workshop constructing an owl as part of the topic on 'night and day'. When he was happy with it he took it to his nursery nurse, Anne, but said nothing to her about his work. She asked him about how the wings worked but he was not forthcoming and said he was taking it home. Wisely, Anne did not pursue the conversation as she knew David well and understood that he needed just to 'check in' his achievements before storing them safely until it was time to take them home. His interdependence was minimal. Kori, who had been watching David's competent use of the stapler, scissors and glue, was keen to explore possibilities of the workshop too. However, at just three, this was only her third day at nursery and she could not make sense of what was on offer. Her ability to ask questions and seek help enabled her to find a more communicative child than David to ask 'what's it for?' and 'how does it work?' questions. Her level of interdependence would continue to be substantial. A setting where more competent children are expected to show responsibility for the newer, younger and less able will provide less confident children with the support they need.

Planning for independent thinking and learning

Independent thinking can be substantially encouraged by planning for resources to be used independently, the theory being that independence of action can lead to independence of thought. During team planning sessions the following resources need to be considered when thinking about autonomy, choice and responsibility:

- space
- time
- people
- equipment.

People

Given the numbers of children in early years settings, it is helpful from a management point of view, as a well as an independence point of view, that an adult does not need to be with all children all the time. For adults to understand their roles, they need to know how the resources listed above can be used most appropriately at any one time. A decision will be made depending on whether children are engaged in self-initiated play or a teacher-led activity or whether observations or assessments are needed. A key feature of successfully supporting young children's independence is the setting up of systems that enable them to manage their own learning on a day-to-day basis. This enables adult interactions to be about what children are thinking about and doing, (the 'shared sustained thinking' we considered earlier and in Chapter 5), rather than doing up aprons and where to put wet paintings. If children can manage their own activities, for example making a model and knowing where to find more glue or where the pencils are to add their name, conversations with adults can be targeted at reinforcing or extending their learning. Similarly, if the expectation of the setting is that areas will be left fit for the next children to use (which initially requires rather a lot of gentle re-enforcement!), adults will not be spending their time tidying the home corner and sweeping up sand. Children's independence is much encouraged if they are able to access the tools they need to keep the setting tidy; they enjoy being in a clean and bright environment and will respect it if there is a culture of pride and ownership.

Apart from the trained adults, it is parents who are the other adults most usually seen in the setting on regular basis. They are a very different resource as they may not be trained in early years practice but bring enthusiasm and a generosity of spirit to their voluntary role. It is vitally important that time is taken to initiate them to the extent of understanding the philosophy which underpins the setting. Some parents' enthusiasm leads them to much joyful cutting, cooking and gluing which results in the children watching rather than taking an active part! Parents' enjoyment of their time spent in early years classrooms does, however, have a really helpful spin-off. If parents have had positive experiences, they will spread the news around the community that they have confidence in their child's setting; this is a far more effective endorsement than any parents evening!

Equipment

Very few practitioners have the luxury of choosing all the equipment they would ideally like. However, the use of equipment can be based on sound principles just like every other aspect of early years provision. If a practitioner believes in valuing children's artistic abilities, then the templates have to go! If settings believe that children need a range of materials through which to explore modelling, then clay must be planned for as well as the play dough (which is far easier to tidy away). If settings really believe in challenging gender stereotyping, then there will be police uniforms and mechanics' overalls for both genders to wear alongside the more gender-specific dressing-up clothes.

Equipment needs to be assessed at least once a year. If a piece of equipment has not been used during that period of time, the chances are that it will not see the light of day again and it needs ruthlessly disposing of. The best equipment is multifunctional, which is why wooden bricks have stood the test of time. Equipment such as wooden bricks needs to be of the best affordable quality and is worth saving up for. However, many items, such as scrap for the workshop area, cost very little but are good value in terms of creativity.

Everyday materials that are in constant use may not be expensive but need to be well maintained. Children will not be drawn to a writing/graphics area where the pencils are always blunt, or want to paint on paper that is curled up at the edges. Paints need mixing freshly each session. Paper must be in good condition and in a choice of shape and colour. If these are on offer, the range of opportunities available to children will be more stimulating.

Table-top toys need to be challenging, for example layered jigsaw puzzles and threading shapes that children have designed themselves. This prevents this area of the provision becoming repetitive and unexciting. Sewing can be a joint activity with groups of children sewing beads, buttons and coloured threads through large pieces of Hessian cloth. The completed work can be used as a wall-hanging, with children eager to talk about what they have done. Photographs which include the children can be used as equipment to great effect, for example in the making of a class alphabet of names or a number frieze.

The workshop, or design technology area, can often be the most creative, with endless possibilities for ideas being tried out and adapted. To encourage independence, organisation is the key to success. As in all areas of the setting, resources need to be well ordered, visible and easily accessible for children to use as they wish. A general rule of resource organisation that seems to work well is to say to children: 'If you can see it, use it, and if you cannot see it, ask.' In this area, small boxes work best for model making. There is not much that anyone can do with large cereal boxes except stick them together. This limits inventiveness somewhat.

Cardboard rolls and egg boxes need storing separately from square boxes so that children can plan what they will make by seeing the range of opportunities clearly and not have to rummage through a muddled selection. Creativity does not easily emerge from muddle and chaos! Small plastic containers with shiny paper, feathers, corks and other collage materials need carefully storing and constantly replenishing to stimulate children's interest. The use of split pins, staplers, scissors, Sellotape and glue needs to be explained to children and only their constant availability will encourage competence. It has to be expected that glue will end up on the floor and Sellotape will be wrapped around table legs. The servicing of these resources needs to be factored into the everyday maintenance of the setting.

Choose as many pieces of equipment as possible that are made of natural materials so that children are given opportunities to experience other options than the practical plastic option favoured by many toy shops. In the same way, children do not need every piece of equipment to be in primary colours. They are quite able to appreciate pale and pastel colours and to enjoy illustrations that are not in cartoon format! The presentation offered by the media and by marketing is another example of how society underestimates young children and often is far removed from independence of thought.

Positive dispositions

Resources, then, need to stimulate children's curiosity and it is this curiosity, combined with the prompting of the sensitive adult, which will encourage positive dispositions towards learning. Dispositions are 'relatively stable patterns of behaviour which are affected by feelings' (Dowling 2000). If a setting consistently provides interesting resources and encourages children to think about them in deep and creative ways, these positive dispositions will become firmly embedded in children's minds. The early years setting has a responsibility to reinforce these dispositions and open up learning opportunities for children so that they believe themselves to be 'can do' people.

Paul and Susannah had been reading John Burningham's book *Time to Get out of the Bath, Shirley* (1978) and very much enjoyed the pages showing kings, queens and knights wearing tabards, crowns and wimples and waving banners. Finding nothing appropriate in the dressing-up area they set about making their own tabards in the workshop. This play lasted many days as they drew round themselves, stapled large pieces of paper together and then decorated them. At the end of each session they asked that their costumes were carefully stored and preserved for the next day. As the play progressed they invented increasingly complex scenarios, at first following the book's storyline but very soon inventing their own rich narratives. At review times they talked about their play and agreed to stage what had, quite soon, become a theatrical performance in front of the whole group. The adults' belief in the principle of encouraging independent thinking enabled Paul and Susannah to develop their creativity alongside their positive dispositions. The enthusiastic response from adults, children and, later, parents, to what had been spontaneous, unplanned play, supported the children in their view that their ideas were valued and worthwhile.

Conclusion

This chapter looks at how children need independence to foster creative thinking and interpendence to support co-operative and collaborative learning. Reassessing the practice in a setting and putting the theory into practice is very challenging. However, an approach which prioritises these issues will do more than anything else to further the learning of the children in the setting.

POINTS FOR REFLECTION

Yourself

The early years practitioner has many roles. What qualities do you feel that you already have and which do you need to develop to fulfil these various roles?

Your practice

How can the practice of you and your team be structured so that the amount that children rely on you is reduced? How can you practically encourage independence and interdependence in the setting?

References

Ball, C. (1994) *The Importance of Early Learning* (Startright Report). London: Royal Society of Arts.

Bennett, N., Wood, W. and Rogers, S. (1997) *Teaching Through Play*. Buckingham: Open University Press.

Bottle, G. (2003) 'Children's mathematical experiences in the home'. Unpublished Ph.D, University of Kent.

Bruce, T. (1992) *Time to Play in Early Childhood Education*. Kent: Hodder and Stoughton.

Burningham, J. (1978) *Time to Get out of the Bath, Shirley*. London: Random House.

Carr, M., May, H., Podmore, V.N., Cubey, P., Hatherly, A. and Macartney, B. (2000) *Learning and Teaching Stories: Action Research on Evaluation in Early Childhood. Final Report to the Ministry of Education*. Wellington: New Zealand Council for Educational Research.

Donaldson, M. (1978) *Children's Minds*. London: Fontana.

Dowling, M. (2000) *Young Children's Personal, Social and Emotional Development*. London: Paul Chapman Publishing.

Fröbel, F. (1826) *On the Education of Man (Die Menschenerziehung)*. Keilhau/Leipzig: Wienbrach.

QCA (2000) *Curriculum Guidance for the Foundation Stage*. London: QCA.

Sylva, K., Melhuish, E., Sammons, P., Siraj-Blatchford, I., Taggart, B. and Elliot, K. (2003) *The Effective Provision of Preschool Education Project: Findings from the Preschool Period*. London: Institute of Education.

Tizard, B. and Hughes, M. (1984) *Young Children Learning*. London: Fontana.

Wood, D. (1998) *How Children Think and Learn*. Oxford: Blackwell.

CHAPTER 9

Relationships

PRINCIPLES . . .

- The relationships that children make with other children and adults are of central importance in their development.

. . . INTO PRACTICE

- Support children's emotional development.
- Be aware of ourselves as models for children's attitudes and develop our skills as partners in learning.
- Value communications with families.

Introduction

The relationships children make with other children and adults are of central importance in their development. This is a well-rehearsed, familiar statement, most often connected with early years settings, where emotional and social learning has been identified as a priority by government and educationalists for many years. While we as practitioners often pride ourselves on the emotional investment we make with the children in our care, research and statistics repeatedly show that exclusion and disaffection pervade our society, even now extending to the youngest in our care. The government's concern for children and their families is reflected in the *Children Act* (2004) which primarily calls on key agencies to work together to safeguard and promote the welfare of children.

We work with children in settings that may be construed as the first formal and key socialising agent, or instrument of society, where children begin to develop relationships in wider groups. As early years professionals, we are charged with playing 'a crucial role in securing children's personal, social and emotional development' (QCA 2000: 29). More than ever, we need to work towards a greater understanding of the way these relationships work. The formation of our earliest relationships is often referred to as 'attachment' (Long and Fogell 1999). To think about these attachment issues in relation to an individual child's sense of emotional well-being will help us build on their existing relationships in an authentic, nurturing way. It will also help us to envisage how a child's sense of well-being impacts on others in an interpersonal way that can affect learning, while also bearing in mind that emotional difficulty can become a significant barrier.

By the time the child is three, four or five years old they will already have engaged in their most formative relationships around their home and will inevitably bring those early experiences of relationship along to the early educational setting (Holmes 2001). So, the quality of any relationship that children are able to make when they enter the larger group of the preschool, nursery or Reception class will be related to the quality of relationship they have already experienced at home. At this time, these comparatively well-established qualities and processes are likely to be about the relationships they have with themselves and with their families. These begin to be communicated physically, emotionally, socially and cognitively from at least the very moment of their birth. Winnicott reminds us of the roots of relationship when he says 'There is no such thing as a baby . . . if you set out to describe a baby, you will find that you are describing a baby and someone. A baby cannot exist alone, but is essentially part of a relationship' (Winnicott 1964).

As practitioners we need to recognise and think about some of these early forms of communication that plant the seeds of relationship, before we can further consider ways of supporting and enabling individual children to work together creatively and collaboratively in an organised learning context in a socially active way (Vygotsky 1934, in Roth 1990).

The story of our lives

When considering the relationships children have with themselves, their families and the growing circle of other children and adults encountered on entering the early years setting, we need to be aware of both internal and external factors as their relationships occur at numerous interrelated levels. It is difficult to deal with these invisible phenomena as they are neither clear-cut nor well defined. The dynamics between individual, internal psychological representations of who we are, and external socio-cultural factors that influence our lives outside the setting, are constantly changing. This means that factors influencing an individual are not fixed but are provisional. In our society, the shape of the family at the beginning of the twenty-first century is a prime example of this changing form.

Enabling engagement and learning

So, how can any child be 'ready for school', a phrase which appears in so many official pamphlets. Surely the settings need to be ready for the child?

To aim towards a more holistic understanding of the reciprocal communication inherent in learning and teaching transactions, we need to recognise the extent to which we are all socially and culturally constructed, and to keep in mind that we also function as teachers and learners in an embedded, interrelational context. As professionals, we need to be aware of the cultures of the child and the setting and also take responsibility for the contribution we bring as individuals. We must recognise the rich opportunities that social and cultural diversity bring. McGuiness (1993) encourages us to think about how these internal and external factors contribute to social functioning. He introduces three interrelated influences:

- **sociogenic** factors: organic, family or environmentally based influences
- **psychogenic** factors: issues of self-image, self-esteem, personality
- **pathogenic** factors: agents that can cause disease such as school ethos, curriculum, teaching styles.

These factors combine to construct the way the child feels about their 'self'. It is to this 'self' that the practitioner responds in the early years setting. In order for practitioners to develop 'warm, interactive relationships' (Sylva *et al.* 2003) with children, they need to be able to unpick and understand how this 'self' is made.

Sustained quality interaction

It is impossible to think about children's behaviour and emotional well-being without also considering what Jeremy Holmes describes as their 'lived experience' with family and friends: 'Like language, emotional life, while being fundamentally biologically based, is learned, experienced and lived in a relational context – a central axiom of the attachment perspective' (Holmes 2001). Often the child's 'lived experience' is artificially divided into a series of separate systems, or compartments, such as school, curriculum, family, friends and home. This helps us deal with practicalities in a logical, rationally structured way and gives us a sense of 'managing' interactions and relations. This is an inadequate approach because it overlooks the complex relatedness of these systems. As Rendall and Stuart (2005) point out: 'a more appropriate and meaningful approach is to find out ways of understanding the complexities rather than reducing them' (p. 17). They suggest a reconceptualising 'systemic approach', an approach familiar to those working in educational psychology. This is an interactionist approach where the setting recognises how its own systems, processes, procedures and activities impact on the learning and teaching transaction. It also considers the diverse, sometimes fragmented experiences children and adults contribute to the whole experience of learning, recognising how each part of the whole is affected by every other part.

Wolfendale (2001), like Rendall and Stuart above, talks about how these systemic and equitable approaches to investment in building relationships with young children and their families pays longer-term dividends for society. Also, projects such as the 'Coram Community Campus' (Pugh 1992), supporting young children and families in South Camden, and the 'SureStart' ethos have helped pave the way for a more joined-up perspective on children's socio-emotional development and learning. This systemic approach will also help us to think about the central issues of inclusion, parent-partnership and the inter-agency agenda of *Every Child Matters* (DfES 2004).

Engaging with these complexities is an emotionally demanding task and may explain why we tend to go for the easy option of managing rather than understanding these influences on relationships systems. The processes involved in building relationships are difficult to discern, think about or consciously engage with. At the same time we all instinctively seem to know that relationships are at the heart, indeed constitute the very human fabric, of our everyday personal, professional and wider social lives.

Ironically, it may be this everyday, 'common experience' perception that can tend to lead some of us towards taking our experience of relationships for granted. It is as though it can be assumed as a wholly natural phenomenon, or even something that 'magically' does or does not happen regardless of efforts to capture, nurture and sustain our own and others' attention. To this extent, the power and value of using time and space to think about as well as to actively engage with children and their families can easily be overlooked in favour of more tangible preoccupations that present as measurable, manageable tasks. This investment of time and space given to understanding the child's emotional life can only enhance the child's learning.

Thomas is five and has behaviour difficulties. Several meetings with his parents followed to support him. We began by considering Thomas's behaviour at bedtime. I suggested an obvious starting place would be to use bedtime routines as an opportunity to talk through issues with Thomas before his bedtime story. This strategy fell flat on its face when Thomas's mother pointed out that as Thomas was no longer a baby he didn't have a bedtime story. This is an example of how listening to the parent's story first, and in depth, was more important than imposing a solution focused on a personal assumption which proved to be incorrect. It also shows the danger of the way that we all inexorably bring our own stories and our own previous relationships to every new situation and relationship we attempt to make. Often, these stories show no respect for professional boundaries.

Relationships are subjective and invisible, not measurable. This means that in settings that have become particularly content laden, ways of developing quality relationships may have been marginalised. Settings that have been concerned with fostering intellectual and academic excellence may have disassociated intellectual growth from emotional learning. We need to realise that effective learning is a holistic experience. Why is it that official recognition of emotional responses is usually only considered when children have difficulties? Does this mean that children who do not appear on the SEN register do not have emotional lives? The exception to this is the Foundation Stage Profile which identifies personal, social and emotional development as an important early years process. But should emotional development stop at six years of age? If so, this supports what Athey (1990) describes as a 'top-down' point of view which 'arises because younger children are seen as less competent than older children'.

How can we, as practitioners, find a way to discern, talk and think about the processes of relationship we experience when working with young children and their families? Emotional responses, though immeasurable, need to be acknowledged so that they will occupy an aptly high status in educational settings. Such settings will prioritise 'bottom-up' learner-centred approaches as a standard issue.

In a multi-agency environment such as that envisaged in *Every Child Matters* (DfES 2004) we do not have a common description or language for emotional learning. Because of the complexities involved in discussing relationships, we must find a discourse or language that ascribes shared meanings for conceptualising issues surrounding children's well-being between health, education and social service professionals. This bridge building would help the relations between disciplines that do not easily, at this time, recognise or acknowledge each other. At such times, we can take heart from a budding bridge builder called Jon, a very creative six-year-old. He struggled with language, especially word-finding . Once, when trying to find the word 'sleeve', he drew on every experience and conceptual association he could summon, took a deep breath and described it quite meaningfully as his 'arm coat'. In order to build bridges between disciplines we need a lot of Jon's lateral thinking.

A framework for thinking about relationships

In our work we need to acknowledge the extent to which we bring *our own selves* when engaging with young children, and to recognise the creative opportunities for learning that reciprocal engagement gives.

In developmental psychology, the relevant research emphasis has generally tended towards considering the developing external relations between mother and infant from birth onwards. However, it is Freud's model of the mind that can perhaps give insights into how external behaviours represent internal states, that is, how children behave represents how they are feeling inside. Bringing together some work of Freud, Klein, Bion and Winnicott, often associated with clinical 'health' settings, with theorists such as Vygotsky who is associated with education, will support an interdisciplinary cross-fertilisation of themes to facilitate multi-agency thinking that is currently being proposed by government.

A central idea of a psychodynamic approach is to do with the relationship between conscious and unconscious states of mind. As Greenhalgh (1994) points out, fairy tales can communicate to the child that struggling against difficulties is an intrinsic part of life. In *Where the Wild Things Are*, Maurice Sendak (1970) imaginatively explores the unconscious tensions and conflicts experienced by the child angered by being sent to bed without supper by a seemingly controlling, unfathomable adult/parental world. This is the same essential world to which he must return after his imaginary adventure with the wild ones, to the only source of love and nourishment he knows and needs. Fantasies such as Sendak's often leave adult readers perplexed as they seek literal and rational meanings. However, this and the popularity of many of his and others' similarly fantastic picture books may indicate the author's ability to tap into the child's unconscious through imagination, to help dissipate unresolved or difficult thoughts and feelings. The child's experience of listening to, or engaging with, the story can be seen as therapeutic. In this way, some aspects of psychoanalytic perspectives may help us to explore emotional factors in learning and teaching about the importance of children making sound relationships with peers and adults.

Although Freud worked with adults, the model of mind he suggested has achieved a human universality that has informed the work of developmental psychology, even to the everyday use and understanding of terms such as 'conscious', 'unconscious' and 'ego'. Freud's model of the mind has three interactive parts:

- the **Id**: represents unconscious, primitive drives towards immediate gratification of biological needs
- the **Superego**: represents preconscious internalisation of socio-cultural demands of parent and family setting
- the **Ego**: represents the conscious maintenance of the self as a whole while adapting to reality; a regulatory mechanism that balances the unconscious demands and conflicts arising from the id and the superego.

Significantly, unconscious and preconscious processes are seen as being to do with the past as the id is associated with primeval states, and the superego's early 'object relations' are informed by first relationships. The stabilising ego then works in a here and now state, to resolve residual past and present conflicts (Thomas 1990). This helps us to see how important it is for the child to develop a healthy sense of 'self' to support a robust ego that is strong enough to weather the perpetual conflicts of the unconscious mind. Ego formation is related to developing a conscious sense of self through active engagement with the environment. This includes the relationships that the child experiences through everyday interactions, initially with parents and family, subsequently with growing groups of friends and professional carers such as teachers.

Winnicott (1971) introduces the useful 'mirror' image when discussing the way the baby first sees themselves in their mother's face. The mirror image describes how the mother reflects her feelings for her baby through facial expression when engaging with the child. It is by this powerful 'holding' function of initially reflecting a consistent image that the mother helps the infant develop an integrated identity. This happens through the process of co-construction as the baby engages in reciprocal patterns of sensory experience through loving play and through eye contact, touch and talk. In terms of supporting the child's sense of self in the early years setting, professionals may model and copy aspects of this notion of 'mirroring' when working with young children. In this way, the practitioner will be engaging in a supportive emotional holding process.

Freud sees the psyche as a dynamic in which the conscious ego oscillates between the pressures of the unconscious id and superego, constantly seeking to maintain psychological balance or equilibrium. As the ego perpetually struggles to establish this state of equilibrium, the ensuing conflict may give rise to neurotic anxieties. The ego attempts to defend the self against excessive anxiety by deploying a range of psychological defence mechanisms such as 'repression', whereby unacceptable feelings are excluded from conscious awareness, and also 'projection', where our own intolerable, painful feelings may be expelled into another.

The smooth running of a humane educational institution relies on creating and sustaining positive relationships via the intra- and interpersonal skills of those involved. We can probably all relate examples of having got rid of unwanted feelings into other people (projection). We have probably also found ourselves in the position of having to 'contain' emotional outbursts from children, parents and or/colleagues. Looking at emotional processes will help us as education professionals by giving useful insights into children's responses and behaviours towards adults and peers. It will also inform our approaches to thinking about, listening to, observing and talking to children and help us to co-construct learning with young children and their parents, which forms the bedrock of developing sound relationships.

While Freud contributed the language and concepts of psychodynamics, it is the work of others, such as Melanie Klein, Wilfred Bion and Donald Winnicott, which particularly focused on earliest childhood development and on the communication inherent in mother–child relationships. This was more familiarly described by John Bowlby (Holmes 1993) as 'attachment theory'. It is aspects of these theorists' work, in particular Bion's concept of 'container-contained', that may be particularly helpful towards identifying important processes in relationships.

Melanie Klein drew on Freud's notion of an internal world of defensive drives, internally constructed to protect the infant from experiencing intense negative emotions. She used this idea to pursue her interest in the area of mother–child relationship that she described as 'object-relations'. Object-relations describe the baby's earliest relationship with a primary carer first experienced by the newborn baby as an object. Gradually, through taking-in or 'introjecting' this good object experience of attentive nurturing, the mother–baby relationship develops, and the baby is more able to tolerate feelings of anxiety experienced in her absence. In this way the mother object gradually begins to emerge as a separate entity. Winnicott's (1964) work helps to illumine Klein when he says that out of 'oneness' with mother, the infant's 'self' gradually begins to differentiate as the mother provides a facilitating environment, engendering the infant's sense of trust and belief in the goodness of the world.

The child's use of what Winnicott describes as a 'transitional object' may signal the child's stage of separation or differentiation of 'self' at the beginning of ego development. Transitional objects often take the form of favoured cuddly toys or comfort blankets to which the child can become particularly attached. This object has the bridging function of symbolising the child's first steps towards emotional independence and thus represents a potentially creative learning space. Winnicott's transitional objects could also be creatively interpreted as a function used by the sensitive early years professional who can aptly tune into the child's 'zone of proximal development' (Vygotsky 1934, in Roth 1990) to develop greater competence and confidence. For example, the practitioner may provide play activities that develop the child's learning. With Adam, who had expressive language difficulties, the transitional object took the form of a scrapbook about himself and his family that we made together. The scrapbook acted as a launch pad for communicative reciprocal interactions not related to the scrapbook, thus enabling engagement and learning to take place.

In stark contrast, excessive anxiety can cause 'regression' which signifies returning to earlier emotional states or behaviours that can be expanded upon by referring directly to the work of Klein (1930). For the practitioner, more accessible examples of regression can be easily brought to mind if we reflect on our own, sometimes irrational behaviours during the most stressful times in our lives. Equally, we can think of the child who, overwhelmed by the demands of large-group activity, may be tearful or may withdraw to a place where solitary thumb-sucking gives greater comfort. Or the child who projects his internal pain or conflict by hurting others or being disruptive when asked to participate in activities they may find stressful. A form of defensive projection that may be particularly useful to understand in educational settings is 'transference'. This occurs when strong feelings about a significant person are unconsciously transferred to another person, with the possible effect in the early years setting that the adult may receive 'projections', or as Greenhalgh (1994) describes: '"catch the flak" originally associated with someone else, most often the children's parents'.

The suggestion, then, is that emergent emotional positions may be psychically revisited at times of stress, or that the ability to deal with anxieties throughout our lives may be connected to our earliest experiences of relationship. This in turn reminds us of the importance of helping young children to develop a strong sense of self which supports a healthy ego to sustain a state of psychic equilibrium. When defence mechanisms such as projection and transference are deployed, it is helpful for us to realise that the child may be unconsciously communicating that they are struggling to process unbearable thoughts and feelings, and the only emotional recourse available to them at that time is pain, avoidance or defensive strategies.

The notion of 'transference' adds further impetus for early years professionals to find ways of working systemically with families to actively promote parent-partnership (Rendall and Stuart 2005). This is done by communicating sympathetically with parents towards understanding children both in and between cultures in a way that acknowledges the interrelatedness of relationships. At a recent conference about child mental health in educational settings, Laura Fruggeri (2005) talked about the relational competence between families and schools, and drew particular attention to the way the relationship between school professionals and parents influences the relationship between children and parents. Once again we see how everything is connected to everything else.

'In every nursery there are ghosts. They are the visitors from the unremembered past of the parents' (Fraiberg et al. 1987: 73). Children will also be affected by their parents' and grandparents' experiences, including those at school. This is called intergenerational transmission, or how relationship experiences or stories or life-scripts may be unconsciously passed through families, sometimes causing confusion and contradiction for the next generation (Holmes 1993).

Wilfred Bion (1897–1979) was a psychoanalyst who became interested in how we survive emotionally. He drew on his experiences as a tank commander during the First World War. Central to Bion's theories is the notion of 'container-contained'. Through the containing process, where the mother is physically and psychologically holding the baby together, the infant experiences the mother containing or making sense of experience for them, and through this first relationship experience the child takes in or introjects a receptive, understanding mother (Coren 1997).

When she is able to soothe and calm by taking-in (introjecting) the fragmented impulses experienced by the newborn infant, she is psychologically holding or containing those feelings for the child in a loving way. She is able to emotionally digest and return those frightened and frightening feelings to the infant in a more tolerable form. This first psychological as well as physically nurturing process of communication he describes as the 'mother's reverie'.

Through this reciprocal container-contained relationship, where the mother initially makes sense of experiences for her baby, the infant gradually begins to develop their own capacity for making sense of, or processing, emotional experience. This experiential, authentic learning process may, for any number of reasons, not always be easy for mother and child to engage with, and many of us may be reassured by Winnicott's (1971) ideas concerning the 'good-enough' mother: 'The good-enough mother (not necessarily the infant's own mother) is one who makes active adaptation to the infant's needs' (p. 10).

However, for Bion it is this containing relationship that engenders a kind of gradual knitting together of inner chaos that is the initial emotional experience that develops the child's ability to think about difficult thoughts and feelings, and therefore initiates symbol formation and makes growth of the mind possible: 'For the baby to turn the sense data of experience into his own reflexive mind, he needs the primary experience of active holding by his mother's mind' (Waddell 1998). In this way Bion (1962) describes what he regards as authentic learning. This requires reflecting on experience to find a way through troubling feelings, rather than avoiding them. While the healthy ego may deploy necessary defences for all of us at times, these defences may also help us to avoid thinking by preventing us from engaging with difficult feelings. This psychological avoidance may also therefore inhibit learning, emotional growth and the capacity for relationship.

In this way, the implications of the 'container-contained' principle for early years practitioners, attempting to build relationships for learning with young children, begin to emerge. If we think successful containment develops emotional tolerance and resilience, and poor container-contained experience can lead to fragmentation in later life relationships, we see how important it is, as Greenhalgh (1994) points out, to respond to young children's communications at a *'relationship* level rather than on a *content* level' (p. 107). As in the mother–child relationship, the early years professional is in a position to provide degrees of emotional containment where they sense children are not ready or able to contain anxieties. The practitioner may equally take opportunities to provide a secure and stable physical and emotional base for containing children who are unable to trust either themselves or others.

Waddell (1998) gives a helpful analogy of containment, or emotional holding, when she describes a child trying to complete a jigsaw puzzle who becomes upset and anxious when unable to complete it. She describes the different responses from different mothers helping the child. One mother may become anxious at her daughter's inability to complete a seemingly simple jigsaw. Her own anxiety is transmitted to the child who becomes similarly anxious and tearful and therefore less able to manage the activity. Another mother may take the matter into her own hands and complete the puzzle for the child, thus taking premature control and affecting the child's sense of personal agency and autonomy. The third mother observes and suggests the child perseveres, carefully judging the level of difficulty while being emotionally available. If the difficulty persists, she moves the jigsaw to help the child match the shape to the space, thus sensitively tuning into what Vygotsky describes as the child's 'zone of proximal development'. In this way, the mother contains the child's frustration and intervenes in an enabling way which promotes the child's sense of well-being and learning. These responses could also be from the same mother responding on different occasions. More relevant to us is that these responses could equally be from different adults supporting such tasks in educational settings.

Of course, as practitioners we also have to bear in mind, just as parents, that in order to contain, we need to have achieved a level of emotional maturity ourselves. As Rogers (1961) points out: 'The degree to which I can create relationships which facilitate the growth of others as separate persons is a measure of the growth I have achieved myself.' If we are aware of our own 'ghosts' (Holmes 1993), we join the emotional playing field equitably and use it as a creative space for communication. This will help us towards more empathic relationships with children and parents.

Building relationships for learning

Even a rudimentary interpretation of psychodynamic approaches such as this chapter offers can help us to reflect on the invisible processes involved in engaging with young children in our care, and to see the importance of reciprocal attunement when nurturing relationships for learning on a day-to-day basis. In educational settings we can easily become too activity centred or product oriented in an effort to channel children's attention towards our own (or others') curriculum agenda. Practitioners must be wary of allowing systems, structures and procedures, particularly in the form of excessive paperwork, to act as a kind of collective, organisational defence against the emotionally demanding and sometimes difficult task of authentically engaging with children. While children undoubtedly need 'a well-planned and resourced curriculum to take their learning forward' (QCA 2000), we must keep in mind that whatever curriculum activity we use, it is the quality of interaction between teacher and child through the process of attentive, sustained engagement that ensures authentic learning.

When we begin to tease out the characteristics of this 'sustained quality interaction', we see how the child will engage when they feel they are being contained by someone who understands the powerful 'holding' potential of relationship processes. Early years staff use observation and listening, making time and creating space for reflection through talk and play. This is because learning is reciprocally co-constructed by child and adult as part of this creative learning and teaching process.

When we understand the value of personal, social and emotional development and prioritise relationships in the educational setting, we truly support a 'bottom-up' model of teaching and learning that values starting from the child and building on the child's existing knowledge, understanding, skills and experience. Reciprocity relies on collaboration, empathy, co-operation and mutual respect. The notions of tuning in to children and working co-operatively with children are exemplified by the early years practice in Reggio Emilia and Te Whariki centres where time and space for working collaboratively are cited as prerequisites:

> Our image of children no longer considers them as isolated and egocentric, does not see them as engaged in action with objects, does not emphasise only the cognitive aspects, does not belittle feelings or what is not logical and does not consider with ambiguity the role of the reflective domain. Instead our image of the child is rich in potential, strong, powerful, competent, and most of all connected to adults and children.

> (Malaguzzi 1997)

In early years settings preoccupied with encouraging children to engage with activities that may rely on the ability to abstract or symbolise, we may see children struggling emotionally. An emphasis on reading or letter formation before the child is ready may lead to anxiety. If we engage with children in the truly 'bottom-up' model through sensitive observation and interaction, we will learn more about when the child is ready to engage symbolically and so make learning more sound.

Conclusion

Relationships in the early years setting are pivotal to learning and teaching. Relationships are about how we communicate with ourselves, our families and others. How we communicate with others depends on how we feel about ourselves. Our 'selves' depend on complex interactions between early attachment experiences and complex socio-cultural processes. Complex processes that deal with context, plurality, subjective qualities that are by definition dynamic, value-laden, provisional and multidimensional are difficult to identify. They are also difficult to talk about or even think about, particularly in a product-oriented, consumer-driven society where education has increasingly become a measurable commodity (Coren 1997).

However, government recognition that effective learning may be strongly linked to personal, social and emotional issues has been recently identified in documents such as *Birth to Three Matters* (DfES 2002) and *Every Child Matters*

(DfES 2004), and supported by the main tenets of the *Children Act*. The latter prioritises the promotion of child welfare through five important outcomes that are to be achieved through active inter-agency work and effective parent-partnership. The aim of joining up health, education and social service professionals sounds promising when aiming for a holistic approach to early years provision, but to initiate a dialogue between parallel professions or disciplines relies, ironically, on a relationship between parties that hitherto have happily ignored one another.

Developing a discourse relies on sharing concepts and meanings behind words, and to this end this chapter has introduced into educational contexts some psychodynamics words and meanings that are more comfortably associated with health settings. Teasing out some psychoanalytic strands from the work of Freud, Winnicott and Bion, directly concerned with processes and qualities of attachment and social and emotional well-being, may help us to think about the way we interact with children. Thinking more specifically about internal functions such as defences which may inhibit learning, together with the importance of containment and emotional holding, may inform our understanding of the relation between emotional engagement, growth and learning.

We also need to keep in mind that children are embedded in the diverse sociocultural dynamics of their own home realities and to begin to understand the way individual children communicate and build relationships. We need to think not only about the child's place in the family, but the family within the child. In a more systemic way, which considers the interrelatedness of experience, we may be able to think about how our relationships with children and their parents affect creative spaces and opportunities for learning.

Tuning in to children socially and emotionally can be a difficult and demanding process which must rely on our own emotional self-attunement. However, to ensure a sound, safe, secure, independent, socially competent future for the children in our care, we must invest ourselves in the principle of sound emotional beginnings. Families provide children's earliest nurturing experiences and, as such, they must be respected and valued.

POINTS FOR REFLECTION

Yourself

Evaluate the personal qualities you have that will help you to develop warm interactive relationships with children.

Your practice

How do you perceive your relationships with children and their families within the setting? Is your relationship with parents on an equal footing?

References

Athey, C. (1990) *Extending Thought in Young Children*. London: Paul Chapman Publishing.

Bion, W. (1962) *Learning from Experience*. London, New York: Karnac.

Coren, A. (1997) *A Psychodynamic Approach to Education*. London: Sheldon.

DfES (2002) *Birth to Three Matters. Framework*. London: DfES.

DfES (2004) *Every Child Matters: Change for Children. Framework*. London: DfES.

Fraiberg, S.H. with Adelson, E. and Shapiro, V. (1987) 'Ghosts in the nursery: a psychoanalytic approach to the problems of impaired infant-mother relationships', in L. Fraiberg (ed.) *Selected Writings of Selma Fraiberg*. Columbus, Ohio: Ohio State University Press.

Fruggeri, L. (2005) Unpublished paper at European Conference for Child and Adolescent Mental Health in Education Settings, Paris, September 2005.

Greenhalgh, P. (1994) *Emotional Growth and Learning*. London: Routledge Falmer.

Holmes, J. (1993) *John Bowlby and Attachment Theory*. Hove and New York: Brunner-Routledge.

Holmes, J. (2001) *The Search for the Secure Base*. Hove: Brunner-Routledge.

Klein, M. (1930) *The Importance of Symbol Formation in the Development of the Ego*. London: Hogarth.

Long, R. and Fogell, J. (1999) *Supporting Children with Emotional Difficulties*. London: David Fulton Publishers.

McGuiness, J. (1993) *Teachers, Pupils and Behaviour: A Managerial Approach*. London: Cassell.

Malaguzzi, L. (1997) 'Experiencing Reggio Emilia', in L. Abbott and C. Nutbrown (eds) (2001) *Experiencing Reggio Emilia*. Buckingham: Open University Press.

Pugh, G. (1992) *Contemporary Issues in the Early Years*. London: Paul Chapman Publishing.

QCA (2000) *Curriculum Guidance for the Foundation Stage*. London: QCA.

Rendall, S. and Stuart, M. (2005) *Excluded from School*. London and New York: Routledge.

Rogers, C.R. (1961) *On Becoming a Person: A Therapist's View of Psychotherapy*. Boston: Houghton-Mifflin ((1967) London: Constable).

Roth, I. (1990) (ed.) *Introduction to Psychology*. Milton Keynes: Open University Press.

Sendak, M. (1970) *Where the Wild Things Are*. Harmondsworth: Puffin.

Sylva, K., Melhuish, E., Sammons, P., Siraj-Blatchford, I., Taggart, B. and Elliot, K. (2003) *The Effective Provision of Preschool Education Project: Findings from the Preschool Period*. London: Institute of Education.

Thomas, K. (1990) 'Psychodynamics: the Freudian approach', in I. Roth (ed.) *Introduction to Psychology*. Milton Keynes: Open University Press.

Waddell, M. (1998) *Inside Lives*. London, New York: Karnac.

Winnicott, D.W. (1964) *The Child, the Family and the Outside World*. London: Penguin.

Winnicott, D.W. (1971) *Playing and Reality*. London and New York: Routledge.

Wolfendale, S. (2001) 'Meeting Special Educational Needs in the early years', in G. Pugh (ed.) *Contemporary Issues in the Early Years*. London: Sage.

Quality

The concept of quality

In Chapter 1 we touched on the complexity of attempting to define what constitutes quality in early years practice. It is a concept that has few certainties and it is currently thought that it may be far more subjective than hitherto acknowledged. Throughout most of the twentieth century, notions of quality were based on an understanding of stages of children's development. This underpinned much western European and North American early years practice and led to certainties that Moss *et al.* described as 'expressing a desire for a clean and orderly world, devoid of messiness and complexity' (Moss *et al.* 1999). The dominant language of a single, uniform set of ideas leads to a perceived ease of assessment of children's progress and the comforting belief that quality provision is assured. It is unlikely that the reality is quite so quantifiable.

While acknowledging that the stages of children's development have a central position in planning a stimulating environment for young children, it is likely that many other dimensions of practice are of crucial importance and it is this range of aspects that we would like to consider when debating the slippery notion of quality. Currently, early childhood educational practice is being set

Children's work valued

among the wider context of a range of services for all children. Documents such as *The Common Core and Key Elements of Effective Practice* (DfES 2004a) have the purpose of bringing practice within the remit of the United Nations Charter for the Rights of the Child and the strategy of *Every Child Matters* (DfES 2004b). The difficulty with this is that, far from being too prescriptive, the statements within these documents are usually too broad to provide clear and purposeful guidelines as there seems to be an overwhelming desire for all parties to be seen to be united on all issues. The search for quality is not served by statements that are generalist any more than it is served by an oversimplistic set of outcome measures.

While the journey continues for definitions of quality, it may be possible to identify certain 'givens' from research that can be accepted as universal. It is possible to define aspects common to all settings that can be considered when asking the question: 'Why is this a good place for children to be?'

Recent research has explored various interpretations of quality but perhaps the one English practitioners will be most familiar with is Pascal and Bertram's quality evaluation framework. This is value based and is to be interpreted using the setting's perception of quality. These dimensions, although subjective, are not

Provision fit for use

arbitrary and were integral to the measurement of quality in the Effective Early Learning Project (Pascal and Bertram 1997). Quality was considered in the following aspects of a setting:

- its aims and objectives
- its curriculum/learning experiences
- the learning and teaching styles
- the ratio of trained staff
- its physical environment
- the relationships and interaction within the setting
- an effective attitude to equal opportunities
- parental involvement, home and community liaison
- the monitoring and evaluation of practice.

Quality practitioners

Given that any judgements made about quality are value laden and will reflect the individual setting's understanding of quality, the key universal thread running through all these dimensions would seem to be the lead practitioner.

This is because it is they who need to be clear about what has to be achieved and how this is to be done. Both the training of the practitioner and their individual personality have huge ramifications for the quality of the practice in settings.

Whether the adult responsible for quality in a setting is called a teacher, manager, practitioner or a pedagogue, what appears to be crucial is that they are trained as an early years specialist. When the Teaching and Development Agency (formerly the Teacher Training Agency) introduced early years as a specialism in Qualified Teacher Status programmes in 1998, trainee teachers were at last freed from having to offer a National Curriculum subject to be accepted onto an early years teacher training course. Training bodies have devised a range of early years specialism courses which include an in-depth knowledge of child development and an understanding of how to teach very young children. It is now generally accepted that specific skills are required by those working within the Foundation Stage and that these skills need to be incorporated within an optimistic and sensitive personality. The combination of attributes required to be an early years specialist can sometimes appear daunting, particularly if the misconception has been allowed to flourish that a love of small children is all that is needed to teach them successfully. Another prejudice seems be one of status, that teaching younger children is somehow an easy option. A head teacher in one school was heard to say that next year the Year 6 teacher would teach in Reception 'as a rest'. The parents of a newly qualified infant teacher were heard to suggest that she might be allowed to teach the older children 'when she was more experienced'.

Margaret Edgington (2004) rightly says that 'Effective teachers make their work look easy'. It is often only when practitioners have been in post for a while that they begin to unpick the complexity of their role. They need to be experts in understanding not only child development but developmental psychology, so as to find ways of teaching that are playful and therefore appropriate for young children. They need the ability to be sensitive both to their pupils and to the family context in which each child is situated. They need to be powerful advocates for the principles which guide their teaching, both within and beyond their setting, and they need a strong physical constitution. They need to be able to organise and manage a learning environment in terms of its space, time and resources and to plan progressive learning and assessment which results in the setting being a place where children and families feel that they belong.

Quality learning and teaching: the curriculum

Learning and teaching are based on curriculum documents that provide broad goals and guidance for practice. In England the early years curriculum is based on the National Curriculum and is focused on the learning and teaching of academic bodies of knowledge. Significantly, the placing of personal, social and emotional development at the forefront of the *Curriculum Guidance for the Foundation Stage* is an acknowledgement that this area of development is 'critical for very young children in all aspects of their lives and gives them the best opportunity for success in all other areas of learning' (QCA 2000). The importance attached to this section of the guidance, together with the advice on using play as a process through which children can learn effectively, reflects the understanding that emotional well-being is a key element of being well educated, a fact incorporated as a central tenet into traditional nursery, or kindergarten, education. Historically, this valuing of emotional well-being was lost during the introduction of the elementary style of working in schools which is so well described by Angela Anning (1997) as being 'based on the notion of social utility – what is useful to teach the sons and daughters of our working classes' (p. 3). It can be argued that the 'skills and drills' approach of elementary schooling is not education at all but rather a mechanism to ensure numeracy and literacy in the workforce (the ideologies of education were discussed further in Chapter 2). Notions of quality, then, are directly related to what is deemed desirable in terms of educational aims and are consequently enshrined in a curriculum that is enforced by law. The battle that has been waging for the last thirty years is a crucial one of ideology and can not be lost if we want to educate children to become creative, imaginative and self-confident adults. Government documents such as *Excellence and Enjoyment* (DfES 2003) and *All Our Futures* (DfES 1999) and programmes such as 'Creative Partnerships' are to be embraced even if their introduction is a sign of how far the pendulum had swung towards a utilitarian system of instruction in our schools. The ideological challenge is set to continue as those charged with implementing the Early Learning Development Framework, which is designed to deliver a single quality framework of services from birth to five by 2008, debate the principles which will underpin it. These principles will need to be carefully designed to safeguard very young children's entitlements to the statements that are enshrined in *Every Child Matters* (DfES 2004b) and *Birth to Three Matters* (DfES 2002). Current headlines in broadsheet newspapers announcing 'Labour's Plan to Educate Toddlers' (*Guardian*, November 2005), when describing the introduction of the Early Learning Development Framework, illustrate only too well the worry that early years practitioners have. They fear that a play-based approach to young children's experiences which safeguards well-being, creativity and independence may not be upheld in the desire to 'avoid mess and complexity' (Moss *et al.* 1999).

Other countries have sought different criteria as the basis of their curriculum rather than academic bodies of knowledge. In New Zealand, the Te Whariki curriculum defines the underpinning strands for children's learning. These underpinning strands are equally concerned with the quality of children's experiences. The strands are typified by a child's question:

- belonging ('Do you know me?')
- well-being ('Can I trust you?')
- exploration ('Will you let me fly?')
- communication ('Do you hear me?')
- contribution ('Is this place fair for us?')

Academic bodies of knowledge are learned and taught in these settings, as is required here, but the child's question which qualifies each strand of the curriculum enables high quality learning and teaching to take place. This is because the child's entitlement and need is at the centre of the curriculum rather than an emphasis on academic knowledge.

A curriculum normally gives guidance as to how learning and teaching should happen. Some, of course, are more prescriptive than others. Te Whariki could be described as more like a framework, in that it states principles but not processes by which the principles should be delivered. The *Curriculum Guidance* that we work to is more directive, with many descriptions of what effective learning and effective teaching look like in practice. While it may be helpful for a new practitioner to be reminded of techniques such as 'using conversation and carefully framed questions because this is crucial in developing children's knowledge', there is a danger that an overprescriptive set of instructions deskills the practitioner and lessens the occasions of spontaneity and fun which are essential in genuine learning. The section of the *Guidance* which describes the steps on the way to the Early Learning Goals and offers suggestions to practitioners of activities that may be used to ensure success, was intended as a supporting document. In other words, it was to be used as a scaffold, to make initial suggestions, and was never intended to be used as a manual. Like all effective scaffolds, it needs to be cast off gradually as the confidence, experience and professionalism of the practitioner grows and they can stand firmly on their own. Used as an occasional reference point it is a valuable tool but it is constraining if used to the exclusion of all other sources of ideas and stimulation.

Quality learning and teaching: the environment

To ensure that quality teaching and learning moves from the pages of curricular documents to the setting, practitioners must move beyond the bare bones of curricular requirements and have the courage to add flesh from:

- professional knowledge of their children;
- professional understanding of how to interpret the curriculum to young children.

This combination of professional knowledge and understanding is a key feature of quality teaching and learning and is essential if children are to be offered the opportunity to make the learning journey that Duffy (1998) categorises as moving from curiosity, through exploration and play to creativity.

Carr *et al.* (2000), in their work on documenting children's progression for assessment purposes, describe a somewhat similar journey from taking an interest, through being involved, persisting with difficulty to taking responsibility.

Another link can usefully be made to Tina Bruce's definitions of children's differing levels of play as being exploratory, representational and free-flow, which we considered in Chapter 2. A learning journey is vital if children are to progress and it is a confident and resourceful practitioner who can join children along the way. Only by ensuring that practical first-hand experiences can offer challenges at a range of learning levels can the setting reassure parents and non early years specialist colleagues that formal paper and pencil is not the only inevitable progression route.

Quality space

The use of space has a considerable influence on the quality of learning that children can achieve. Cramped, disorganised and, therefore, undervalued play spaces probably do more than anything else to give the message to children that nothing much is expected in terms of learning. It cannot be too strongly stated that, given a generous amount of space, children will be able to create imaginative places, complex plots and ingenious solutions to problems. Thankfully, the value of the outdoor space has now been embedded in Foundation Stage practice and it is a truism that, with the possible exception of information technology, there is no learning that happens indoors that cannot happen outside. There is, though, much outside learning that cannot happen inside, such as digging, large-scale den-making, climbing, searching for mini-beasts and trail-making. Organisations such as the Forest Schools and Learning Through Landscapes have been influential in bringing the potential of outside learning to the fore and they have built on an already proud tradition of the kindergarten garden. It is outside that many young children feel that they can develop their independence, as it is here that their most valued achievements are likely to happen. When a small child shouts with enthusiasm, 'Look what I can do!', it is usually a physical achievement such as jumping, climbing or running that they are celebrating. In the Foundation Stage it is expected that the outside area is used in just the same way as the inside; the same expectations for learning and behaviour are in place and some Ofsted teams refer to it as the 'outside classroom'. The idea that the outside is somewhere to 'let off steam' and 'run around' may hold true further up the school but in the Foundation Stage the outside is where the child can explore, reflect and learn in just the same way as indoors but with added dimensions of much more space and a wider range of stimuli.

Quality time

The fact that deep-level learning does not happen in a hurry is a concern in an age that Guy Claxton (1997) has described as one where the philosophy of 'think quicker, we need the results' predominates.

Both Jacquie Cousins, in her book *Listening to Four-Year-Olds* (1999), and Williams and McInnes, in their book *Planning and Using Time in the Foundation Stage* (2005), have expressed the anxiety of many practitioners that young children's educational experiences are being severely compromised by lack of time. Cousins' descriptions of children no longer building tall castles because of lack of time to finish them should give us all cause for concern. This means that we are not offering children enough time to learn in any depth or to practise and return to learning, the process that enables children to securely embed a concept in the mind. Children like Sarah who was described at the woodwork bench in Chapter 1 will never become proficient at the small motor skills involved in her play if she only has a few minutes at the woodwork bench and if it is only available occasionally. When the team plan the optimum use of resources in the setting, it is vital to think through what aspect of the session needs the most time and why. Is it necessary, for example, for children to begin their day on the carpet, waiting for latecomers so that the register can be called? Would it be possible for a system of adult-checked self-registration to allow children to come into the setting and get engaged on the activities that they may well have been planning on the way?

How necessary is it that all children join together for snack time? Could children be trusted to know when they are thirsty and to help themselves to water when they know they need it? The practice of giving Foundation Stage children slots in the hall for PE or in the computer suite cut down still further the uninterrupted length of time that they need to become engrossed in deep-level learning. Sometimes it is easy to get swept along by whole-school policies which may suit older children very well but are not appropriate for the youngest children. The promotion of independence is not well served by the chunking of time into small fragments because it militates against children being able to make decisions about how to spend their time. 'Time', as Jack said in Jacquie Cousin's book, 'is as long as it takes' (Cousins 1999). This may be an idealised view but it is one that wise practitioners would do well to work towards.

Time is a precious commodity; its use must be thought through carefully. Priority should be given to things that are the most important to children, such as exploratory learning. The least amount of time needs to be apportioned to those things that adults sometimes feel are important such as registration, getting children dressed and undressed for PE sessions, moving large groups of young children around the building and organising frequent whole-group times. These activities are often intimidating to young children who do not understand their purpose and, by their nature, tend to teach dependence rather than independence. Believing in the principle of independence requires us to trust that children can and will organise their time effectively, given adequate resources and supportive adults. When observing children organising their own play within a context of good quality resources and a generous time-frame, it is clear that very young children can, and do, initiate and sustain their own complex and challenging learning for long periods of time.

Quality ethos

The children's questions quoted above from *Learning and Teaching Framework* (Carr *et al.* 2000) seem to us to be very good places to start when considering universal aspects of high quality provision. They echo the positive attributes of young children, their potential to make contributions to their settings and to persist with challenge and uncertainty, while respecting their vulnerabilities, such as the need for a safe and fair environment in which to flourish. They also reflect children's entitlement under *Every Child Matters* to, for example, be healthy and the right to be in a place where they can 'enjoy and achieve'.

Any setting which seeks to be a good place for young children might ask their own questions about how to put these rights and entitlements into practice. The questions in the sections below would act as a guide.

Do all the adults know what they are meant to be doing at any time of the day, and why?

The timetable for each day needs to be clear in the minds of all adults in the setting. Close co-ordination is essential if large numbers of young children are to be successfully taught in ways which allows them freedom of choice and autonomy. Some adults will be working on adult-initiated activities with individual children or small groups. These activities may be tightly planned and have learning objectives which will be monitored. Other adults will be moving around child-initiated play, extending it, observing it and facilitating it. They may also be assessing children's learning through their play or modelling aspects of role play or offering language to support children who find joining play situations challenging. Even the setting organised to encourage child-initiated learning, which requires uninterrupted periods of time and a flexible use of resources, has to be tidied up and children gathered in from a wide range of places and activities. Those who do this regularly know that to achieve this calmly and effectively can be challenging and one member of staff whose children are still clearing away the bricks when everyone else is singing the 'Goodbye' song can quickly become very unpopular!

Is the setting ready in good time each morning so that staff feel and look in control of what is happening?

When families arrive at the start of a session the setting needs to look ready for the children who will use it. Often a brief meeting is held before families arrive to ensure that all staff members know their responsibilities for the day, know of any special activities, observations, birthdays or other events and are clear about the organisation of group times. They should be aware of what is in the outside area and provision that children may wish to extend or vary based on its previous use. Pencils need to be sharp, supplies of paper, paints and crayons checked and dressing-up clothes looked at each day for missing buttons or broken zips. The provision offered must be attractive, well organised and fit for use. This also encourages a higher level of play as children will respond to clean and well-cared-for equipment by treating it with respect.

Are there interesting things to look at and to do?

A provision-based setting relies on the principle of capturing children's innate curiosity and developing their positive dispositions to learn by providing opportunities for children to become engaged with what is provided so that they may make the learning journey that we considered earlier. Interesting things to look at and do will encourage children to take an interest, become involved, persist with challenge and difficulty, express a view and take responsibility. If there is nothing exciting in the setting there will be nothing to engage with, persist with, express an opinion about or take responsibility for. A dull place where children are not engaged will encourage disaffection and the possible long-lasting belief in children that this is not a place for them and that education, or school-type learning, is not for them either. If we are asking children to struggle with challenges and the uncertainties of new learning we must give children interesting things with which to struggle.

Are all parents and children welcomed personally each session? Have staff time for a short conversation with carers and do they recognise the importance of this?

This is an organisational issue but requires belief in the principle that parents are children's first and enduring educators and must be equal partners in their education. It may be challenging on a day-to-day basis but if children have key workers, or an adult is responsible for a particular group of families, this task becomes manageable and pays huge dividends in terms of understanding the needs of families, and contributes to working within the context of a supportive community. Families and carers will always support settings which have time to listen to concerns. Staff need to be able to identify between conversations which can be conducted briefly on entry or exit and those which require listening to in more detail at mutually convenient times.

Is children's work valued: are photographs displayed and is there an attitude of the children being the most important element of the setting?

The staff's response to children's endeavours sends profound messages both to families and to children themselves. Settings where adults are genuinely interested in children's models, drawings, writings and paintings will react to children's enthusiastic cries of 'Look what I've done' with sensitivity. This will lead to their asking questions about the process of construction such as 'Which bit did you do first?', which is a question the child can think about in depth. Very often young children's creations are about the process of making rather than the end-product and conversations about the process make much more sense to them. This is well illustrated by an incident in a state nursery class which was undergoing an Ofsted inspection. On his clipboard the inspector had the question 'Does the child know the purpose of the activity?' and so asked Simon, aged four, what he was making at the woodwork bench. Simon, who had been working hard for ten minutes at sawing the end off a large piece of wood, knew that his reply was particularly important but he was not, in fact, 'making' anything. Lost for a suitable reply, his gaze fell to the floor; he then smiled broadly up at the inspector and replied 'Sawdust'.

Misinterpretation of children's learning can be greatly eased by the use of explanatory photographs of the possible learning outcomes of different areas in the setting. They also act as an aide-memoire to children who may be new to provision-based learning. Possible ideas on which to build are helpful in the development of their own critical thinking skills. Photographs play a useful part in the process of record keeping and can be a valuable part of scrapbooks that children make on leaving a setting to inform their next class of their strengths and interests.

Is the environment clean and tidy and organised, but not to the extent that experimentation or accidents are frowned upon?

If we are going to expect children to be independent learners there must be systems in place so that they can manage their own activities. As we mentioned in Chapter 6, children benefit from being expected to manage some aspects of their daily routine. These would include clearing away, washing paint pots and being able to organise their model making from start to finish by understanding how to use the equipment, select resources and name and store the finished product. They need initial and probably ongoing support to achieve complete independence but most children, by the end of the Foundation Stage, are capable of a high level of autonomy in the day-to-day business of organising themselves. A belief in the principle of independent learning will help practitioners recognise that mistakes will be made during this process and that spilled paint, glue and water are a part of that learning process. Flexible thinking is also messy but a glance in an artist's or potter's studio is a helpful reminder that it is not only children's creativity that grows out of apparent muddle. There is a fine, but crucial, dividing line between flexibility and chaos!

Are children spoken to courteously, their requests and grievances acted upon and their views taken seriously?

The attitudes of adults towards each other reflect the culture of the setting. This culture permeates the atmosphere and sets the expectation that if parents and carers are listened to, then so, also, will children be. Children's attempts to persist with problems and to concentrate and succeed are significantly affected by the response of adults to their struggles. It is in an environment in which they are consulted and listened to that they will achieve most highly. Children do have genuine grievances and the wise practitioner will spend as long as it takes supporting the aggrieved child. The practitioner can offer strategies and words to empower them in difficult situations. It is usually aspects of relationships on which children need advice and the early years setting is performing a valuable role if children at this early stage are enabled to conduct social and emotional relationships in assertive, considerate and thoughtful ways.

Do ALL the adults working in the setting know the philosophy underpinning what they do every day and do they realise that they must share the manager's values to provide children and parents with a continuity of attitude?

The pedagogical underpinning of the setting and the principles by which the staff teach need to be shared so that there is a united response to children and their families. Basic understandings about confidentiality and health and safety will need reiterating to adults who come into the setting at every level. This will encompass factors such as high handles on doors, safe use of climbing equipment and tools. Adults who regularly spend time helping in the setting will need guidance at a more professional level, such as how to support children's independence, how children are spoken to and the behavioural expectations. They will need to be made aware of the confidential nature of professional conversations about children's progress. It is during these conversations that parent helpers will gain an understanding of the high levels of thoughtfulness that go to make up the quality of ethos and values that are an intrinsic part of a good setting.

Does the manager know the reasons behind everything that happens in the setting and is he or she able to respond readily to parent questioning?

Part of the role of management is to question every aspect of the setting for which they are responsible. It should be possible to ask oneself the question 'Why are those children doing that?' or 'Why is that equipment in that place?' and for there to be a sound educational reason based on the principles by which they teach. If the truthful answer to the question 'Why are there more table-top toys out on a Friday afternoon?' is that staff want to leave quickly at the end of the session, then the likelihood is that the quality of learning is being compromised. It is profoundly sad to see paint pots washed up and chairs on tables a full half-hour before the children leave because not only does this reduce their learning opportunities but it gives the message that adults' interests are valued more highly than those of the children.

Is the pattern of the session easily understood by parents and children? Does it provide continuity while being flexible?

Routine is a double-edged sword! It is necessary for children and adults to be able to find what they need and know how long they have in a session and it undermines children's ability to get deeply involved in learning if the setting is constantly being rearranged in the interests of novelty. Imagine trying to bake a cake in a kitchen where the contents of the grocery cupboard were always being moved to other cupboards and the flour was never where it was last time it was needed! Children need the stability and continuity of being able to predict some certainties on which to base their ideas and creativity. They will not commit themselves to a deep level of learning in an environment that does not offer this consistency. On the other hand, routines must be there to support and enable learning and not to constrain it by being inflexible and dominant. Parents and carers also need the stability of knowing exactly what is happening when, but will accommodate the occasional variation in routine for events such as celebrations and festivals which provide opportunities for enjoyment and merrymaking!

Quality leadership and management

Reflected throughout this chapter is the notion that the more effective the setting is in providing high quality learning experiences, the easier it all appears. Colleagues who are not specialists in early years sometimes think that working with the youngest children is easier than teaching children in Years 1 and 2. However, in our experience of teacher education, it is the weaker students who begin to flounder when they realise the range of skills they need to develop successfully in order to manage the dynamic and flexible nature of the Foundation Stage setting and then to lead the team with confidence.

Even if the manager and the leader of the early years team are the same person, it is important to distinguish between the two roles. Management concentrates on the organisational responsibilities of making an early years setting work effectively. Leadership, however, requires a visionary aspect that can ask the bigger questions such as 'Which principles underpin our setting?', 'What do we need to change? Why and how should this be done?' and 'Is our team working together?' And 'Does everyone feel that their contribution is valued?' These 'big' questions need to be asked through whole-staff evaluation at regular intervals if the setting is to be a dynamic and positive workplace for its staff.

The early years leader has the responsibility to *achieve the task* of leading and managing by:

- using principles which are backed by research;
- defining the task and forming priorities.

Building the team is best approached by:

- explaining the practice;
- inviting suggestions.

Developing individual staff members' talents is vital and can be achieved by:

- using interpersonal skills;
- recognising and using the strengths of each individual within the team.

Working with and leading the professional team requires the leader to establish a relationship that is just that, professional. It is based in the workplace and founded on mutual respect which does not need to spill over into life outside the setting but which often deepens into friendship. The leader needs to be even-handed with members of the team, recognising that they all have different strengths, concerns and needs which have to be sensitively considered. The time and effort taken to build up relationships within the early years team is a profoundly worthwhile and rewarding undertaking as there is much companionship and enjoyment to be had in working with colleagues who share the enthusiasm of seeing children making progress and who genuinely trust each other and enjoy working together. Children and families sense this happy atmosphere and the setting becomes a 'good place to be'.

Conclusion

This chapter has looked at some of the elements of quality that define a setting as being a fit place for young children to flourish. It has considered different curricula and the effects that pedagogy and culture will have on how quality is perceived. Quality is, by its nature, subjective, but not arbitrary; we have suggested aspects of quality that are universal. These include the personality and training of practitioners and the importance given to the considerations of the resources of time and space that are at the disposal of the team. One of the most important elements of the good setting is the ethos, the 'feeling' that one experiences both as a visitor and as a stakeholder, and this proves hard to define. One is reminded of the analogy of the elephant as being very hard to describe but instantly recognisable when encountered! When high quality is achieved, the early years setting is a joyful place, humming with engaged and reflective children, and where practitioners can take pride in the fact that they are having a profound influence on the lives of the children and families who share in the daily life of the setting. It is also a place where the adults feel challenged and enriched.

POINTS FOR REFLECTION

Yourself

When you think about high quality practice, which elements do you consider being important?

Your practice

How can your setting be organised so as to support each level of children's play, from exploratory to free flow?

References

Anning, A. (1997) *The First Years at School.* Buckingham: Open University Press.

Carr, M., May, H. and Podmore, V. (2000) *A Learning and Teaching Framework.* Wellington: New Zealand Council for Educational Research.

Claxton, G. (1997) *Hare Brain, Tortoise Mind.* London: Fourth Estate.

Cousins, J. (1999) *Listening to Four-Year-Olds.* London: National Children's Bureau.

DfES (1999) *All Our Futures.* London: DfES.

DfES (2002) *Birth to Three Matters. Framework.* London: DfES.

DfES (2003) *Excellence and Enjoyment: A National Primary Strategy.* London: DfES.

DfES (2004a) *The Common Core and Key Elements of Effective Practice.* London: DfES.

DfES (2004b) *Every Child Matters: Change for Children. Framework.* London: DfES.

Duffy, B. (1998) *Supporting Creativity and Imagination in the Early Years.* Buckingham: Open University Press.

Edgington, M. (2004) *The Foundation Stage Teacher in Action.* London: Paul Chapman Publishing.

Moss, P., Dahlberg, G. and Pence, A. (1999) *Beyond Quality in Early Years Education and Care: Postmodernist Perspectives.* London: Routledge Falmer.

Pascal, C. and Bertram, T. (1997) *Effective Early Learning.* London: Hodder and Stoughton.

QCA (2000) *Curriculum Guidance for the Foundation Stage.* London: QCA.

Williams, J. and McInnes, K. (2005) *Planning and Using Time in the Foundation Stage.* London: David Fulton Publishers.

Author Index

Subject Index